AMAZING
ENTREPRENEURSHIP
UNLEASHED:
From Self-Discovery to Success

By David Phung M.S.

Published by Book Writer Corner
www.bookwritercorner.com
433 Walnut Ct Pittsburgh
PA 15237, USA
Phone: (878) 219-4793
email: info@bookwritercorner.com

Book Title: AMAZING ENTREPRENEURSHIP
UNLEASHED: From Self-Discovery to Success
eBook ISBN: 978-1-960815-86-6
Paperback ISBN: 978-1-960815-89-7
Hardcover ISBN: 978-1-960815-88-0
Printed in USA
Book Designed by Book Writer Corner
Book Cover by Book Writer Corner

This book is Dedicated to My Parents, Dad and Mom. My wife, Amanda, and our Daughter, Katie. Along with our Agents, Producers, and Associates.

In addition, this book is dedicated to the dreamers who defy convention, the doers who transform visions into reality, and the relentless spirits forging paths through uncharted territories. It honors those who see entrepreneurship as a pursuit and a way of life—a journey of self-discovery, innovation, and unwavering determination.

Contents

ENDORSEMENT

Hi David.

I am honored that you shared your book with me.

I have not read the entire book yet but everything that I have read has been compelling and inspiring. Especially reading about your early struggles in Utah. I think that people who look at success rarely ever get to appreciate how much unglamorous hard work that went into that success. I think one of the greatest hurdles to entrepreneurship is the need to feel safe. The greater the goal the greater the risk and many people choose safety over risking a chance for great success.

You're writing is inspiring and reminds me of Earl Nightingale. My favorite quote is:

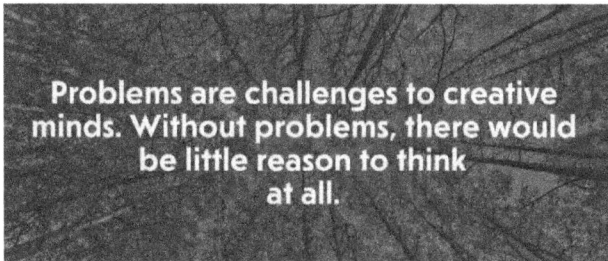

> Problems are challenges to creative minds. Without problems, there would be little reason to think at all.

Jin Hwang | Analyst Technology Services Practitioner | Nationwide

The book is really good David! the title speaks for itself. **Amazing**.

Vino Ruiz | Chief Executive Officer | Aroha Curis Employment Services

Great Entrepreneur Book; well written and informative.

Peter Wu, MD | Family Doctor | Sacramento CA

Wow, that's impressive!

Jenny Trac | ERS Premier | Strong Insurance Services International

Very good job!

Andrew Lan | *President* | *Sacto Press*

"In this insightful book, David Phung shares a compelling journey of personal and professional growth, having immigrated from Vietnam at the age of 12. With a foundational start in insurance at Nationwide, the narrative delves into various roles in insurance sales, emphasizing the advantages of this career path. The author skillfully breaks down entrepreneurship across different sectors and imparts wisdom on maintaining balance as an entrepreneur, drawing parallels with Darwinism and highlighting entrepreneurship as synonymous with independence. Chapter 3 provides a realistic portrayal of entrepreneurial challenges, offering a valuable outline of diverse business directions. The "15 Ds of entrepreneurship" encompass practical advice, emphasizing the strategic use of finances and continuous adaptation to a dynamic market. The book integrates personal experiences seamlessly, emphasizing the importance of vision, teamwork, and building meaningful connections. With a focus on sales and scaling, it serves as an excellent guide for entrepreneurs at all levels, offering high-level concepts in a realistic and relatable manner. Overall, it's a must-read for both beginners and seasoned veterans in the entrepreneurial landscape."

Thank you for sharing this with me and allowing me to share my thoughts. I am a true believer in always sharpening your tools and never staying complacent. This book is a great reminder of that; I loved your storytelling's realistic aspect.

Charles Stehli | *Regional Director* | *Account Services Coventry*

Dear David,

I am so very proud of you. Your book is so impressive. I can tell you really put your heart and soul into this book through your journey, especially after everything health insurance agents go through in the past and currently.

Your book is going to be my map and guide to survival of writing my book. Below is a part of my book on agents and agencies. I am sure you can relate most to this section.

I believe in the power of education. I am so fortunate to have your book in my arsenal of wisdoms going forward. It applies to many aspects of the health care industry. As this information comes to me naturally a lot of times without thinking after 2 decades in the health care industry, it does not for others, a road map and guide was certainly was in need to be more efficient and organized. I am so thankful for you.

Amy Canchola MHA | Individual | Family Medicare Senior Sales Executive
Anthem, Inc

This book is very organized and succinct.

Michael R. Jensen | Mortgage Loan Originator | NEXA Mortgage

This is a good reference point for people considering starting their path as a business owner. David has experience and insight as a person who has been there. David provides a checklist of essential components in private enterprise. David delivers a realistic viewpoint for motivated employees to be successful.

Carl Tomaselli | SBA loan officer and investment advisor | Referral agent for
Sotheby's

"AMAZING Entrepreneurship Unleashed: From Self-Discovery to Success" by David Phung is a compelling and motivational book highlighting the importance of perseverance and resilience in the entrepreneurial journey. It inspires and serves as a practical guide, offering actionable steps and a tangible roadmap for individuals looking to understand and apply the practical aspects of entrepreneurship. What sets it apart is its commitment to being more than just a theoretical guide, making it a hands-on, practical handbook for those venturing into the world of entrepreneurship.

Dorcas Yee | Business Owner | Self-Employed Marketing Director

Great book in simple explanation by David Phung.

Jatinder Singh | Security Consultant | Secure plus

This book is a great book for a person who is starting an insurance business, which breaks it down in steps.

Jack Chu | Insurance Advisor | Self-employed Advisor

As an entrepreneur, I find this book very informative and worth reading. After reading David's book, I got some insightful ideas and tips for building my own business. I recommend this book to anyone considering leaving their corporate jobs and wanting to pursue becoming their own boss!

Jenny Trac | Broker Owner | Strong Insurance

This is an Awesome book, five stars.

Cyndi Luu | Real Estate Agent | KW Vaca Valley

It is fantastic a book.

Vira Egli | Account Manager | Record Guardian Technologies Inc.

The book is nicely written.

Eddy Cheung | Account Manager | LEE KUM KEE (USA) Foods, Inc

The book looks good. The information is easy to understand.

Paul Srirattan | Insurance Advisor | Worldwide Wealth Insurance Solutions, LLC

BEST BOOK YET!

Honda Nguyen | Entrepreneur | From Honda

INTRODUCTION:

Entrepreneurs are made but not born

It is a myth to believe that Entrepreneurs are born; the truth is that entrepreneurs are made by being committed to taking risks and persevering against all odds. As entrepreneurs, it's likely we'll make mistakes along the way; success comes from learning from our own mistakes through our journey.

Setting Expectations and Piquing Interest

Entrepreneurship is a beacon of opportunity in a world that embraces innovation, celebrates bold ideas, and rewards those who dare to tread the beaten path. It's the realm where dreams become businesses, ambitions are woven into the fabric of reality, and the indomitable human spirit takes flight. This is a world where fortunes are made and lost, innovation and determination collide, and the unquenchable thirst for success drives individuals to push the boundaries of what's possible.

Welcome to "Entrepreneurship Unleashed: From Self-Discovery to Success," authored by David Phung. David, a self-made entrepreneur, arrived in the United States from Vietnam at the age of 12. He embarked on a remarkable journey, one that led him to work with insurance companies, where he gained invaluable knowledge and skills. However, David's story is not merely one of learning but one of applying that knowledge with unwavering determination. Through years of hard work and an unrelenting desire to succeed, David established his own business, breathing life into the principles and strategies that are the heart of this book.

As we begin this exploration of entrepreneurship, we recognize the heart and soul of those who take this path, the individuals who dare to challenge the status quo, and the relentless optimists who believe in their dreams even when the world remains skeptical. But it's more than just a path; it's a mindset, a way of life, a boundless journey where self-discovery is entwined with innovation, risk is mitigated by preparedness, problems become stepping stones to triumph, and resilience is the cornerstone of every victory.

This book is your guide, mentor, and companion on the exhilarating quest for entrepreneurial success. We will traverse the realms of the entrepreneurial mindset, unveil the secrets of self-discovery, and delve into the art of risk management. You'll learn to navigate challenges with a problem-solving prowess, draw inspiration from the stories of triumphant entrepreneurs, and craft a vision that propels you forward with unwavering determination. We'll guide you through the intricate process of building your support network and mastering the arts of sales and marketing. You'll discover the keys to scaling your venture, expanding it globally, and ultimately leaving a lasting legacy.

But this is not just a book about theory and concepts; it's an action handbook. It's a blueprint for those who seek not only to understand entrepreneurship but to embrace it wholeheartedly, to dive into the deep waters of innovation, and to emerge stronger, wiser, and more successful.

The following chapters are more than words on a page; they are the roadmap for your entrepreneurial journey. Whether you're an aspiring entrepreneur or a seasoned business owner, this book has something for you. It's designed to provoke thought, inspire action, and provide the necessary success tools. The path ahead is paved with challenges, but countless stories of triumph also illuminate it. As you venture further into the pages of "Entrepreneurship Unleashed," you'll understand that your determination, refusal to give up, hard work, and burning desire for success are the building blocks of a prosperous entrepreneurial future.

So, with your dreams in your heart and this book in your hands, let's embark on this incredible journey. The world of entrepreneurship is calling, and it's time to answer.

1 EMBRACING REALISM: A JOURNEY OF INSPIRATION

"Entrepreneurship Is Not Just About Creating A Business; It's A Mindset That Turns Challenges into Opportunities, Setbacks into Stepping Stones, And Dreams into Reality."

As I reflect on my entrepreneurial journey, I invite you into the heart of my distinctive approach to business—an approach rooted in realism, empathy, and a profound appreciation for the individuality of each person. This chapter unveils the transformative stages of my life, from the vibrant streets of Vietnam to the entrepreneurial landscape of the United States, and how these experiences laid the foundation for my success.

What Inspired Me to Write the Book?

The inspiration to write this book stems from a deep-seated desire to share my success story and the resilience, resourcefulness, and belief that anyone can build a brighter future through entrepreneurship. This book caters to a diverse audience—those seeking strength, existing entrepreneurs seeking reinforcement, and individuals who may not yet see themselves as entrepreneurs but could benefit from embracing an entrepreneurial mindset.

In the following chapters, we'll delve deeper into the elements and traits constituting a successful entrepreneur or business owner. Join me as we explore the entrepreneurial mindset and learn from a realistic entrepreneur who embodies the spirit of hard work, dedication, and an unwavering commitment to success.

Welcome to a journey of inspiration—welcome to the pages of "Entrepreneurship Unleashed: From Self-Discovery to Success."

INTRODUCTION TO 3 TYPES OF ENTREPRENEURS:

Entrepreneurs come in various forms with distinct skills, strengths, and focuses. Understanding the different types of entrepreneurs provides insights into their contributions to the business landscape. Here are three primary types:

1. **Creator:** The Creator entrepreneur is driven by innovation and creativity. Their focus lies in generating new ideas, concepts, and products. These entrepreneurs excel at identifying gaps in the market and devising unique solutions. They are passionate about bringing novel concepts to life and are often involved in the early stages of product development.

2. **Builder:** Builder entrepreneurs thrive on scaling and growing businesses. They are adept at taking existing ideas, refining them, and establishing scalable systems and processes for growth. These entrepreneurs are instrumental in transforming startups into sustainable and profitable enterprises. Builders are strategic thinkers who understand how to effectively structure and expand a business.

3. **Operator:** The Operator entrepreneur excels in executing and managing established systems. They are skilled at optimizing day-to-day operations, ensuring efficiency, and maintaining stability within a business. Operator entrepreneurs often step in after the initial phases of a company have been set up, bringing discipline and structure to ensure smooth ongoing operations. Their focus is on managing and improving existing processes for long-term success.

THE REALIST ENTREPRENEUR:

In the world of entrepreneurship, I've chosen a less-traveled path that doesn't conform to a one-size-fits-all mentality. I see beyond mere sales transactions, valuing the unique qualities of each individual. My commitment to serving fellow humans has been the cornerstone of my success, drawing many to seek guidance and recommendations.

TYPES OF SOCIAL ENTREPRENEURS:

Social entrepreneurs are individuals who leverage entrepreneurial principles to address social issues and create positive change. Within this field, various types of social entrepreneurs emerge, each with a unique focus and approach. Here are four distinct types:

1. **Community:** Community-based social entrepreneurs focus on positively impacting a specific locality or community. They identify local needs, collaborate with community members, and develop solutions tailored to address the unique challenges faced by those in that area.

2. **Non-Profit:** Non-profit social entrepreneurs establish organizations that address social issues. Their primary goal is to create positive change rather than generate profits. They rely on funding, donations, and grants to sustain their initiatives and often collaborate with stakeholders and other non-profits to maximize their impact.

3. **Transformational/Builder:** Transformational or builder social entrepreneurs are visionary leaders who aim to bring about large-scale, systemic change. They focus on transforming entire sectors or industries, creating sustainable solutions that have far-reaching impacts. These entrepreneurs often work on policy changes, innovative business models, or large-scale initiatives to

drive transformation.

4. **International/Cross-Border:** International or cross-border social entrepreneurs operate globally, addressing social issues that transcend national borders. They navigate diverse cultural, political, and economic landscapes to implement solutions that can have a broad and lasting impact. These entrepreneurs collaborate with organizations and stakeholders from different countries to address complex global challenges.

CHARACTERISTICS OF AN ENTREPRENEUR:

Entrepreneurs possess a unique set of characteristics that contribute to their success in the dynamic world of business. Here's a brief introduction to nine key traits that define an entrepreneur:

- **Don't Take No for an Answer, always follow up, Try Again and Again:**
  Entrepreneurs are persistent and resilient. They face rejection with determination, learning from setbacks, and relentlessly pursuing their goals.

- **Learn from the Best, Expert, or Experienced Coach:**
  Successful entrepreneurs are continuous learners. They seek knowledge from experts, mentors, and experiences, using each opportunity as a valuable lesson to enhance their skills.

- **Stay Hungry and Ambitious:**
  A perpetual hunger for success and unyielding ambition is characteristic of entrepreneurs. They strive to achieve more, set higher goals, and consistently strive for excellence.

- **Never Stand Still and Wait for Opportunity:**
  Entrepreneurs are proactive and seize opportunities. They don't wait for success to come; instead, they

actively create and pursue opportunities to propel their ventures forward.

- **Don't be Afraid to Knock Doors:**
  Fearlessness is common among entrepreneurs. They embrace challenges, boldly knocking on doors for business opportunities, partnerships, or networking.

- **Not Shy Selling or Make Cold Calls:**
  Entrepreneurs excel in salesmanship. They are comfortable promoting their products or services, making cold calls, and engaging in direct sales activities to drive business growth.

- **Build Long-Term Business Relationships in Your Network:**
  Networking is a cornerstone of entrepreneurship. Successful entrepreneurs build and nurture long-term relationships, recognizing the value of a strong professional network for mutual growth and support.

- **Inspire and Motivate Those Around You:**
  Entrepreneurs possess leadership qualities that inspire and motivate their teams. They create a positive and dynamic work environment, fostering innovation and dedication among their collaborators.

- **Believe in Your Faith and Gut Instinct:**
  Trusting one's instincts and having faith in decisions is crucial for entrepreneurs. They rely on their intuition to make strategic choices, confidently navigating uncertainties.

These key characteristics collectively define the entrepreneurial spirit, showcasing the determination, resilience, and leadership required to succeed in the competitive business landscape.

ENTREPRENEUR PERSONALITY TRAITS:

IGNITING SUCCESS IN BUSINESS

Entrepreneurship is not merely about starting a business; it's a journey that demands unique qualities. Successful entrepreneurs often share certain personality traits that set them apart in the competitive landscape. These eight traits, handpicked by entrepreneurs themselves, encapsulate the essence of what it takes to thrive in the business world.

- **Future Vision:**
  Entrepreneurs are keen to envision possibilities beyond the present, seeing opportunities where others may see challenges.

- **Good Work Ethic:**
  Diligence and a strong commitment to hard work are foundational traits driving entrepreneurs to persevere through challenges and dedicate themselves to achieving their goals.

- **Resilience:**
  In the face of setbacks, entrepreneurs exhibit remarkable resilience, bouncing back from failures with newfound strength and determination.

- **Winning Mindset:**
  A positive and competitive mindset propels entrepreneurs forward, fostering a continuous pursuit of success and a refusal to accept defeat.

- **Confidence:**
  Entrepreneurs exude confidence, not only in themselves but also in their ideas and ventures. This self-assuredness attracts support and fuels bold decision-making.

- **Positive Attitude:**
  Maintaining a positive outlook, even in adversity, enables entrepreneurs to navigate challenges optimistically,

inspiring themselves and those around them.

- **Forward Thinker:**
  Entrepreneurs are forward thinkers, anticipating trends and staying ahead of the curve. This trait enables them to innovate and adapt to an ever-evolving business landscape.

- **Passion and Burning Desire to Succeed:**
  At the heart of every successful entrepreneur is an unwavering passion and an intense desire to succeed. This burning ambition fuels their persistence and fuels their journey toward achieving their business goals.

A JOURNEY OF TRANSFORMATION EARLY YEARS:

My story begins with a remarkable journey—a journey not just across continents but a transformation of life itself. Moving from the vibrant hustle of Vietnam to the serene landscapes of Salt Lake City, Utah, marked a profound shift. With unwavering determination and a strong entrepreneurial spirit, my parents instilled in me the values of education, hard work, and responsibility. These values became the bedrock of my work ethic and perspective on life.

A CRUCIBLE OF LEARNING FIRST JOB IN THE INSURANCE INDUSTRY:

Before entering the insurance industry, I navigated diverse roles, from washing dishes in a Japanese restaurant to after-school cleanup jobs. These early experiences taught me the essence of diligence and perseverance, where success demanded hard work, dedication, and the ability to overcome challenges.

My tenure as a Customer Services Representative and Claim Processing Specialist at the Employment Development Department in Oakland, California, became a crucial learning ground. Adopting a consultant's approach, I listened to clients, offering thoughtful solutions with empathy, strong listening skills, patience, and attentiveness. These interactions earned me the trust and gratitude of clients—a testament to the humanistic approach that underlies my entrepreneurial journey.

A LEAP OF FAITH THE DECISION TO START MY OWN BUSINESS:

In 2006, a significant decision led me to join Nationwide Insurance as an agent, marking a new chapter in my career. Equipped with skills honed in customer service and claim processing, the pivotal turn in 2008 prompted me to start my own agency—a leap of faith demonstrating courage and determination to take control of my entrepreneurial path.

CHOOSING INSURANCE CAREER CHANNELS/OPTIONS:

Choosing an insurance career opens up various channels and options, each with unique characteristics and opportunities. Here's a brief introduction to three primary career channels in the insurance industry, along with specific sectors within each category:

Independent/Brokerage:

Independent insurance agents or brokers work with multiple insurance companies, offering a range of products to their clients. This channel provides flexibility and the ability to tailor coverage to individual needs.

- **Private Sector:**
  Independent agents can work in the private sector, serving individual clients, businesses, or other private entities. This option allows for a diverse clientele and a broad range of insurance products.

- **Corporate Sector:**
  Independent brokers may also focus on corporate clients, providing insurance solutions for businesses of various sizes. This often involves creating comprehensive coverage plans tailored to corporate needs.

- **Government/Non-Profit Sector:**
  Some independent agents may specialize in serving government entities or non-profit organizations, addressing their unique insurance requirements.

Captive/Exclusive:

Captive insurance agents work exclusively with one insurance company. While they lack the flexibility of offering products from multiple providers, they often have access to in-depth training and support from their affiliated company.

- **Private Sector:**
  Captive agents in the private sector focus on serving individual clients or businesses, representing the products and services of a single insurance company.

- **Corporate Sector:**
  Captive agents may work exclusively with corporate clients, aligning their services with the specific insurance offerings of their affiliated company for businesses' needs.

- **Government/Non-Profit Sector:**
  Some captive agents may specialize in providing insurance solutions exclusively to government agencies or non-profit organizations.

Multi-level marketing (MLM):

In the MLM model, individuals build a team and earn commissions from their sales and the sales generated by their recruited team members. This model is less traditional in the insurance industry but has gained some traction.

- **Private Sector:**
  In the private sector, MLM involves selling insurance products directly to individuals or businesses while recruiting and managing a sales team to expand the business.

- **Corporate Sector:**
  MLM structures may exist within the corporate sector, where agents focus on corporate clients and build teams to maximize sales and recruitment.

- **Government/Non-Profit Sector:**
  While less common, MLM structures could potentially be applied in providing insurance solutions to government or non-profit entities, leveraging a network of agents.

Choosing a specific career path within these channels depends on individual preferences, career goals, and the desire to work in the private, corporate, or government/non-profit sectors. Each option offers unique advantages and challenges, providing ample opportunities for growth and success in the insurance industry.

INSURANCE COVERAG:

Insurance is a vital aspect of risk management, providing financial protection against unforeseen events and potential losses. Our agency offers a comprehensive range of insurance coverage to address diverse needs and risks faced by individuals and businesses. From safeguarding personal assets with auto, home, and umbrella insurance to providing specialized coverage like flood and earthquake insurance, our agency aims to offer tailored solutions. Additionally, our commercial insurance offerings encompass various aspects such as commercial auto, bonds, business insurance, errors and omissions (E&O), and cybersecurity insurance. Individuals can also explore life insurance, annuities, accident insurance, disability coverage, long-term care, and travel insurance for comprehensive protection. This section outlines the spectrum of insurance options available through our agency, highlighting the diverse coverage areas designed to meet our clients' specific needs.

BENEFITS OF BECOMING AN INSURANCE AGENT

Entering the insurance industry unfolded several advantages that shaped my entrepreneurial journey:

1. **New Commission:**
   Earning commissions on policies sold provided a direct financial incentive.

2. **Residuals:**
   Policies like life insurance offered residuals, ensuring a stable income stream.

3. **Minimal Capital Investment:**
   The industry required little initial capital investment, making it accessible.

4. **Flexibility:**
   The ability to work from anywhere aligned with the growing remote work trend.

5. **Sole Proprietorship:**
   Operating as a solo entrepreneur provided full control over business operations.

6. **Job Security:**
   Entrepreneurs can create their job security by taking control of their professional destinies. They are not subject to the whims of corporate decisions or restructuring.

7. **Long-Term/Dependable:**
   Building a successful business can provide long-term and dependable income, especially when the venture is well-

established and has a solid customer base.

8. **Autonomy:**
Entrepreneurs enjoy the freedom to make independent decisions, allowing for greater control over their business direction and strategies.

9. **Flexible/Remote:**
Entrepreneurship often allows for flexible work arrangements, including the possibility of working remotely. This flexibility is valuable for achieving a better work-life balance.

10. **Chance to Build a Career or Business to Meet Your Needs:**
Entrepreneurs can align their careers or businesses with their personal values, goals, and lifestyle preferences.

11. **Growth and Development:**
Building and managing a business fosters continuous personal and professional growth. Entrepreneurs are constantly challenged to adapt, learn, and innovate.

12. **Management Control:**
Business owners have full control over their management strategies, enabling them to implement changes swiftly and efficiently without bureaucratic hurdles.

13. **Economic and Development in the Community:**
Successful businesses contribute to the economic development of their communities by creating jobs, supporting local suppliers, and driving economic growth.

14. **Improvement of Living:**
Entrepreneurship can lead to an improved quality of life, providing financial stability and the ability to invest in personal and family well-being.

15. **Association with Like-Minded Individuals:**
Entrepreneurs often find themselves surrounded by a

network of like-minded individuals, creating opportunities for collaboration, shared experiences, and mutual support.

These benefits, coupled with my entrepreneurial spirit, were instrumental in my decision to pursue a career as an insurance agent and start my own agency.

PERSONAL EXPERIENCES FROM THE INSURANCE INDUSTRY

Handling Rejection:
Reflect on the personal experience of venturing into the insurance sales industry amidst warnings of its competitiveness. Despite skepticism, confidence and hard work became allies. In any crowded field, uniqueness prevails—different personalities and tailored philosophies cater to diverse audiences. Believe in yourself, follow your instincts, and success, with a well-thought-out plan, is achievable and inevitable.

Building A Support Network:
Understand the pivotal role of a support network comprising mentors, peers, and advisors. This network offers guidance and encouragement during challenging times, creating a robust foundation for sustained resilience.

Neighbors:
Neighbors form an immediate support network, often readily available for assistance or camaraderie. Building positive relationships with neighbors fosters a sense of community and provides a local support system.

Acquaintances:
Acquaintances are individuals with whom you have some familiarity but may not know deeply. Cultivating these connections can expand your network and create opportunities for mutual support.

Friends:

Friends are individuals with whom you share a deeper connection, trust, and mutual understanding. They provide emotional support, advice, and companionship, contributing significantly to your well-being.

Friends Of Friends:

Expanding your network to friends of friends broadens your circle and introduces new perspectives. These connections often serve as bridges to different social and professional opportunities.

Local Connections:

Establishing connections within your community, beyond immediate neighbors, can lead to a more extensive support network. This might involve engaging with local businesses, organizations, or community leaders.

Community Events And Gatherings:

Participating in community events and gatherings provides opportunities to meet new people, share experiences, and strengthen connections. These events create a sense of belonging and offer platforms for networking.

Interest Groups:

Joining interest groups based on hobbies, passions, or professional interests connects you with like-minded individuals. These groups offer a shared sense of purpose, often resulting in strong, supportive relationships.

Meetup Groups:

Meetup groups provide platforms for individuals with common interests to come together. Whether for professional networking, socializing, or pursuing hobbies, Meetup groups facilitate the expansion of your support network.

DARWIN'S SURVIVAL RULE:

Darwin's Survival Rule posits that survival is not determined by strength but by adaptability and fitness.

Darwinian Law:
Darwin's principles state that inherited characteristics, prolific reproduction, and offspring fitness are crucial. Similarly, entrepreneurs inherit knowledge, skills, and connections, contributing to their ability to tackle operational challenges.

Understanding Darwinism:
In simple terms, Darwinism, a theory of biological evolution by Charles Darwin, applies to entrepreneurship. Like in the natural world, where species evolve through natural selection, entrepreneurs face challenges, and only a few endure, emphasizing the need to navigate various variables for success.

Survival Of The Fittest Theory:
Known as natural selection, this theory highlights that adaptation is key for survival in challenging circumstances. This reflects the heightened competition where businesses strive to stand out in the competitive business landscape.

The 4 Rules Of Darwin:
Darwin's four propositions include prolific reproduction, struggle for existence, variation within a species, and the tendency for offspring to inherit parental traits. These principles align with the challenges and hereditary aspects of entrepreneurship.

Five Principles Of Darwin's Theory:
Natural selection, characterized by Variation, Inheritance, Selection, Time, and Adaptation (VISTA), can be paralleled with entrepreneurship, where startups inherit challenges that require daily problem-solving.

80/20 Rule (Pareto Principle)
The 80/20 rule, applicable to business and economics,

suggests that 20% of causes lead to 80% of outcomes. This principle resonates with the success rate in entrepreneurship, where a minority achieves significant success.

Substantiation – How Many Years Entrepreneurs Last:
Data indicates that only 25% of new businesses survive beyond 15 years. This underlines the notion of survival of the fittest in entrepreneurship.

Average Age Of Entrepreneurs:
The study reveals that successful startup founders are typically between 35-45 years old, emphasizing the importance of experience in entrepreneurial success.

Business Degrees:
Entrepreneurs often opt for business degrees, such as strategy, operations, and finance, as they provide a comprehensive overview essential for successful business ventures.

Entrepreneurial Challenges:
Most entrepreneurs struggle due to a lack of the right ideas, knowledge, and information to make informed decisions. Proper research and diligence can help them avoid pitfalls.

Law Of Large Numbers:
In probability and statistics, the law of large numbers states that as a sample size grows, it means we get closer to predicting the average of the entire population's outcome. The larger the numbers, the closer we predict the reality or sum.

Industries like insurance, financial, investment, casino, voting, etc., use large numbers to reach better outcomes or expected probabilities. Entrepreneurs can apply the law of large numbers in their venture if they see fit.

BALANCING WORK, ENTREPRENEUR, OR YOUR BUSINESS

Balancing work, entrepreneurship, or running a business with personal aspects of life is crucial for overall well-being and sustained success. Here's a brief introduction to key elements in achieving this balance:

- **Family:**
  Balancing work with family involves allocating time and attention to maintain meaningful connections with loved ones. Prioritizing family ensures a supportive foundation and contributes to a holistic sense of fulfillment

- **Physical and Mental Health:**
  Maintaining good physical and mental health is essential for productivity and happiness. This involves incorporating healthy habits such as regular exercise, sufficient sleep, and stress management into daily routines.

- **Exercise:**
  Regular physical activity is integral to maintaining optimal health and energy levels. Incorporating exercise into a busy schedule not only enhances physical well-being but also contributes to improved focus and resilience.

- **Recharge Energy/Reset:**
  Taking time to recharge and reset is vital for preventing burnout. This could involve short breaks during the workday, weekends off, or periodic vacations. These moments of rejuvenation help maintain enthusiasm and creativity.

- **Leisure:**
  Balancing work with leisure activities provides mental and emotional relief. Engaging in hobbies, pursuing interests, or simply relaxing contributes to a balanced and fulfilling life.

- **Stress Relief:**
  Street relief, or stress relief, is essential for managing the pressures of work and entrepreneurship. Techniques such as mindfulness, meditation, or engaging in activities that bring joy can help alleviate stress and maintain a positive mindset.

- **Social Activity:**
  Incorporating social activities into a busy schedule fosters connection with friends and the community. Whether through social events, gatherings, or networking, maintaining a social life contributes to a well-rounded and enriched lifestyle.

Balancing these elements requires intentional effort and effective time management. Striking the right balance ensures sustained productivity, prevents burnout, and contributes to overall life satisfaction. Recognizing the interconnectedness of personal and professional aspects allows individuals to build a harmonious and fulfilling life.

Chapter Summary

"Embracing Realism: A Journey of Inspiration" unfolds a unique approach to entrepreneurship rooted in realism, empathy, and appreciation for individuality. Reflecting on a transformative life journey from lively streets in Vietnam to the U.S. entrepreneurial landscape, the realist entrepreneur prioritizes service, drawing others seeking guidance. The narrative spans early life lessons, career shifts, and the decision to start an insurance agency in 2008, detailing the diverse career channels within the insurance industry. It explores the benefits of becoming an insurance agent and offers insights into achieving a balance between work, entrepreneurship, and personal life. The chapter concludes with a profound commitment to entrepreneurship as a path to empowerment, inspiration, and overcoming challenges— a prelude to the comprehensive exploration of entrepreneurial traits in subsequent chapters. Welcome to "Entrepreneurship Unleashed: From Self-Discovery to Success."

2 UNLEASHING THE ENTREPRENEURIAL SPIRIT

"In the unpredictable journey of entrepreneurship, thorough preparation is the compass that guides you through the challenges and opportunities, ensuring your success."

Welcome to a transformative chapter where we embark on a journey of self-discovery and personal development, unlocking the potential that lies within you. As a seasoned entrepreneur, I recognize the profound impact of self-evaluation and growth on the road to success. Join me as we delve into the critical aspects of unleashing your entrepreneurial potential.

Why Entrepreneurship Matters?

My commitment to entrepreneurship extends beyond personal success. It is a powerful path for individual empowerment and a solution to modern challenges. It transcends the insurance industry; it's a path that inspires and guides others in building their businesses, achieving financial independence, and making valuable contributions to their communities.

The values instilled by my parents, the journey from Vietnam, early job experiences, and tenure in the insurance industry converged to create a robust foundation. Entrepreneurship, for me, is about allowing individuals to seize control of their destinies, create opportunities, and surmount obstacles. It's not just about my triumph; it's about empowering others to follow their entrepreneurial dreams.

INGREDIENTS OF SUCCESSFUL ENTREPRENEURSHIP:

Embarking on the journey of entrepreneurship requires a well-crafted recipe for success. Just as a chef combines various ingredients to create a delectable dish, an entrepreneur must blend key elements to ensure a thriving venture. The six essential ingredients that form the bedrock of successful entrepreneurship are:

- **Good Ideas:**
  At the core of any successful business is a unique and viable idea. Entrepreneurs must be adept at identifying market needs, devising innovative solutions, and presenting ideas that resonate with their target audience.

- **Strong Leadership:**
  Leadership is the guiding force that steers a business toward success. Entrepreneurs need to exhibit qualities such as vision, decisiveness, and the ability to inspire and motivate others. Strong leadership sets the tone for a resilient and dynamic enterprise.

- **Great Team:**
  No entrepreneur can navigate the complexities of business alone. Building a capable and cohesive team is crucial. A team that shares the entrepreneur's vision, complements each other's strengths, and works synergistically is key to overcoming challenges and achieving milestones.

- **Well Planning:**
  Successful entrepreneurship involves meticulous planning. Entrepreneurs must map out their business journey, set clear objectives, and develop strategies to reach their goals. A well-thought-out plan serves as a roadmap, guiding the business through various stages of growth.

- **Execute Business Strategy:**
  Planning alone is insufficient; execution is paramount. Entrepreneurs need the ability to implement their strategies effectively. This involves making informed decisions, adapting to changes, and consistently moving forward in line with the established business strategy.

- **Maintain Growth:**
  Beyond initial success, sustaining and expanding a business is crucial. Entrepreneurs should focus on maintaining growth by identifying new opportunities, optimizing operations, and staying attuned to market trends. Continuous improvement and adaptability are key to long-term success.

NAVIGATING THE MAZE:

Choosing the Right Legal Structure for Your Business in the US and UK

Building a successful business starts with laying a strong foundation, and choosing the right legal structure is a crucial first step. Both in the US and UK, entrepreneurs have a variety of options, each with its own set of advantages and considerations. Let's navigate the legal landscape of these two common business environments.

United States:
- **Sole Proprietorship:** Simple and inexpensive, but you hold unlimited personal liability for your business.

- **Partnership:** Share ownership and profits with partners, but all partners are also personally liable for the business's debts and obligations.

- **Limited Liability Company (LLC):** Offers personal liability protection, flexibility in management structure, and pass-through taxation (profits and losses pass through to personal tax returns). Can be taxed as a corporation if desired.

- **Corporation (S-Corp, C-Corp):** Separate legal entity from the owner(s), offering limited liability protection but with more complex paperwork and filing requirements. S-Corp has pass-through taxation, while C-Corp pays corporate taxes with double taxation (corporate profits taxed first, then dividends to shareholders taxed again).

United Kingdom:

- **Sole Trader:** Similar to the US Sole Proprietorship, offering simplicity but with unlimited personal liability.

- **Partnership:** Joint ownership of the business, with shared profits and responsibilities, but also shared personal liability.

- **Limited Liability Partnership (LLP):** Offers personal liability protection for partners, similar to a US LLC, but with specific regulations for certain professions.

- **Private Limited Company (Ltd):** Separate legal entity from the owner(s), offering limited liability protection and a more formal structure with directors and shareholders. More complex filing requirements compared to other options.

Choosing the right legal structure requires careful consideration of several factors:

- *Liability:* How much personal risk are you willing to take?

- *Taxation:* How will profits and losses be taxed?

- *Administration:* What level of complexity and paperwork are you comfortable with?

- *Growth Potential:* Does the structure accommodate future growth plans?

Understanding the legal implications of each option empowers you to make informed decisions that align with your unique business goals and vision. With the right foundation, you can navigate the complexities of running a business and increase your chances of long-term success.

ELEMENTS IN ENTREPRENEURSHIP:

Entrepreneurship is a multi-faceted journey that involves various stages and elements. Here are three essential elements in the entrepreneurial process:

Identifying Entrepreneurial or Business Opportunities:
One of the foundational elements of entrepreneurship is the ability to identify viable opportunities. Entrepreneurs keenly observe the market, industry trends, and gaps in existing solutions. They seek innovative ideas, emerging technologies, or unmet needs that can serve as the foundation for a new business venture. Identifying opportunities requires a combination of market research, creativity, and a deep understanding of customer needs.

Planning and Preparing the New Venture:
Once a promising opportunity is identified, entrepreneurs engage in comprehensive planning and preparation. This involves developing a business plan that outlines the new venture's mission, vision, target market, value proposition, and operational strategies. Entrepreneurs consider financial projections, risk management, and resource allocation during this phase. Effective planning is crucial for laying a solid foundation and securing the resources needed for the venture's successful launch.

Planning the Venture and Taking Appropriate Action:
Beyond the initial planning, entrepreneurs continuously refine their strategies and take appropriate actions to execute their plans. This involves making critical product development, marketing, team building, and financial management decisions. Entrepreneurs must be agile and

responsive to changes in the market and adapt their plans accordingly. Taking deliberate and well-informed actions is essential for steering the venture toward success and navigating the dynamic landscape of entrepreneurship.

HARD WORK, DAY IN, DAY OUT:
THE GRIND OF ENTREPRENEURSHIP

The glamour often associated with entrepreneurship belies the core truth—it demands unwavering commitment and hard work, day in and day out. In this chapter, we dive into the essence of the entrepreneurial grind. A relentless work ethic marks my journey, and now, I share the habits and strategies that drive success. Success rarely comes overnight; it is the culmination of consistent effort, dedication, and persistence to navigate challenges. Learn how to persevere through tough times and establish daily routines that propel you toward your goals.

1. Balancing ambition with patience

Ambition fuels the entrepreneurial spirit, compelling us to reach for the stars. Yet, in the pursuit of greatness, balancing ambition with patience is equally crucial. Drawing from my own experiences, we explore the delicate synergy between setting high goals and maintaining patience. Discover the fine line between persevering and allowing things to unfold in their own time. This chapter provides insights into setting ambitious targets and cultivating the patience required for long-term success.

2. Perseverance weathering the storm

Every entrepreneurial journey encounter storm, but the unwavering resolve to weather challenges defines success. In this chapter, we delve into the indispensable role of perseverance. Drawing from my challenges and triumphs, I explore strategies to navigate the storms with resilience. Discover the mindset and practices that will keep you steadfast in pursuing your goals, ensuring that adversity becomes a stepping stone toward success.

3. Cultivating a growth-oriented mindset

Building on the growth mindset introduced in the previous chapter, we now dive deeper into cultivating this mindset, which is crucial for personal development. Explore strategies for adaptation, continuous learning, and evolution as you progress in your entrepreneurial journey. Cultivating a growth-oriented mindset is not just the key to success but the foundation for sustained excellence. Join me as we uncover the mindset shifts and practices that propel you toward continual growth and success.

SELF-EVALUATION AND PERSONAL DEVELOPMENT

At the core of entrepreneurial success lies self-awareness, a compass guiding us through the dynamic landscape of business. In this chapter, we embark on the essential practice of self-evaluation. Discover the importance of recognizing your strengths, acknowledging weaknesses, understanding passions, and delineating goals. The entrepreneurship journey begins with a deep understanding of oneself, a driving force that has propelled my success. Learn how self-awareness catalyzes personal and professional growth, setting the stage for your entrepreneurial endeavors.

- **Work Ethics:**
  Work ethics encompass principles and values that guide one's behavior in a professional setting. This includes integrity, accountability, and a strong work ethic, all of which contribute to a positive and productive work environment.

- **Time/Dedication:**
  Success often correlates with the commitment of time and dedication to tasks. Understanding the demands of a role or business venture and being willing to invest the necessary time and effort is crucial for achieving goals.

- **Commitment:**
  Commitment involves a steadfast dedication to one's responsibilities and objectives. It implies a readiness to overcome challenges and stay focused on long-term goals despite possible obstacles.

- **Expertise/Special Skills:**
  Possessing knowledge and special skills relevant to the field enhances one's ability to excel. Continuous learning and honing specific skills contribute to professional growth and proficiency.

- **Experience:**
  Experience brings a wealth of knowledge and a deeper understanding of industry dynamics. Whether through hands-on work or exposure to diverse situations, experience is a valuable asset that often translates into better decision-making.

- **Niche:**
  Identifying and specializing in a niche area can set individuals apart in a competitive landscape. Focusing on a specific niche allows for a more targeted approach, catering to a particular market segment or need.

- **Goal-oriented:**
  A goal-oriented mindset involves setting clear objectives and developing a strategic plan to achieve them. This forward-looking approach helps maintain motivation and provides a roadmap for success.

- **Connection:**
  Building and maintaining meaningful connections within one's industry or professional network is essential. Networking can open doors to opportunities, collaborations, and valuable insights, contributing to personal and professional development.

THE GOLDEN RULES IN BUSINESS:

- **Prioritize Relationships:** Success in business, like in any endeavor, hinges on relationships. Both personal and business connections should be nurtured and valued. Recognize that business thrives through people and their relationships. Cultivating strong bonds with clients, vendors, peers, and community members is essential. Treat others as you wish to be treated, and remember, people are the lifeblood and engine of your business.

- **Invest in People:** Understand that the strength of your business lies in the people associated with it. When individuals, whether clients or employees, feel valued and respected, they become ambassadors for your brand. Their endorsement and word-of-mouth referrals can significantly contribute to your company's growth. Build lasting relationships and witness the successful rewards of your efforts.

- **Long-Term Vision:** Look beyond immediate gains and focus on establishing enduring relationships. A strong foundation of trust and goodwill pays dividends in the long run. Building rapport with stakeholders contributes to sustained success, creating a positive cycle of referrals and business expansion.

INTRODUCTION TO BUSINESS LOCATION:

Selecting the right location for a business is a strategic decision that can significantly influence its success. The choice of business location is a multifaceted process that involves careful consideration of various factors, each playing a crucial role in shaping the venture's performance. Entrepreneurs must weigh aspects such as accessibility, target market proximity, competition, and regional regulations to ensure the optimal positioning of their business. A well-chosen location can enhance visibility, attract the target audience, and contribute to operational efficiency. This section will explore the key considerations and factors involved in the decision-making process for business location.

Safety/Risk Assessment: Entrepreneurs face a myriad of challenges related to safety and risk, ranging from natural disasters to criminal activities. A comprehensive safety and risk assessment involve evaluating potential threats and adopting measures to mitigate and prevent adverse impacts on business operations. Entrepreneurs should research the chosen location and its surroundings to understand short-term and long-term risks, including nearby fires, storms, floods, hurricanes, tornados, earthquakes, and other natural disasters. Proactively factoring these risks into business operations and expenses is crucial.

Wild/Brush Fire Score: In the context of a changing climate, the rise in wild/brush fire incidents is a concern for businesses. Entrepreneurs need to assess the wild/brush fire score of their chosen location, categorized as low, moderate, high, or extreme. A high brush fire score not only poses immediate safety risks but may also impact business insurance rates and coverage placement. Entrepreneurs must consider these factors to make informed decisions about the safety and sustainability of their business in a specific location.

Crime Rate Score: The crime rate in a chosen location significantly influences business viability. Higher crime rates pose challenges for business operations and can impact insurance considerations. Insurance carriers often assess crime rate scores before extending coverage, and a high crime rate may result in difficulties in obtaining coverage or increased insurance costs. Entrepreneurs must carefully evaluate crime statistics and their potential impact on the safety and security of their business.

Loss Prevention /Mitigation: Loss prevention is a critical aspect of business management, encompassing prevention, awareness, compliance, detection, investigation, and resolution. Particularly relevant in a retail environment, entrepreneurs need to adopt targeted loss prevention measures to address issues like burglary, theft, and mischief. Implementing robust loss prevention strategies enhances the overall security of the business and minimizes the risk of financial losses.

THE IMPORTANCE OF LOCATION IN BUSINESS

Just as my journey unfolded from the dynamic streets of Vietnam to the entrepreneurial landscape of the United States, the location of your business significantly shapes your entrepreneurial path. Adaptability to different environments played a pivotal role in my success, and now, I share insights into choosing the right location for your venture. Explore strategies to understand the market, turn geographical challenges into opportunities, and adapt effectively. Assess the suitability of your chosen location and discover how it can become a strategic advantage in your entrepreneurial journey.

THINGS TO CONSIDER WHEN CHOOSING A LOCATION

When selecting a location for a business, several factors come into play, each influencing the success and viability of the venture. Here's a brief introduction to key considerations when choosing a location:

1. **In a Trade Area:** A trade area ensures proximity to suppliers, potential business partners, and industry-related resources. This can facilitate efficient logistics and foster collaboration within the business ecosystem.

2. **Proximity to the Consumer Market:** The closeness to the target consumer market is crucial. It reduces transportation costs, enhances customer accessibility, and allows for a better understanding of local preferences and trends.

3. **Business Community:** The presence of a thriving business community can provide networking opportunities, shared resources, and a supportive environment. This sense of community can contribute to the growth and success of a business.

4. **Close to Talent Pools:** Access to a pool of skilled and qualified workers is essential for business operations. Choosing a location near educational institutions, industry-specific training centers, or a skilled workforce can be advantageous.

5. **Low Cost:** Cost considerations encompass factors such as rent, utilities, taxes, and other operational expenses. Choosing a lower-cost location can contribute to improved profit margins and financial sustainability.

6. **Convenience:** The convenience of the location for both customers and employees is a critical factor. Factors such as parking availability, public transportation access, and overall ease of navigation contribute to the convenience of the location.

7. **Close to Major Centers and Streets:** Proximity to major centers and streets enhances visibility and accessibility. A location near busy thoroughfares or commercial hubs can attract more foot traffic and potential customers.

8. **Remote Operations:** Since Pandemic, entrepreneurs, business owners adopted to working remotely, rent increase, operating expense, with advance in technology, delivery service, remote work has become common among startups and new age enterprises. Talk about this because this is the trend, also congest traffic on the road,

freeway, cut travel time, is the way to go.

When making decisions about the location of a business, it's essential to conduct thorough research and consider the unique needs of the specific industry and target market. Balancing these considerations ensures that the chosen location aligns with the business's goals, maximizes opportunities, and contributes to long-term success.

Join Us on the Journey

As we navigate this chapter, consider it an invitation to unleash your potential. Understand yourself, your environment, and the importance of consistent effort. Together, we explore the fundamental building blocks of entrepreneurial success, providing actionable insights to apply to your journey. So, let's begin the journey of unlocking your potential as an entrepreneur. Welcome to a chapter that sets the stage for your personal and professional transformation.

Chapter Summary:

"Unleashing the Entrepreneurial Spirit" is a transformative journey into self-discovery and growth. The seasoned entrepreneur underscores the pivotal role of self-evaluation, emphasizing strengths, weaknesses, and goal-setting. Crucial components like work ethics, dedication, commitment, expertise, experience, niche focus, goal orientation, and networking are explored. The chapter delves into the significance of choosing the right business location, offering insights into trade areas, consumer proximity, business communities, talent pools, cost considerations, and convenience. The harsh reality of the entrepreneurial grind is revealed, emphasizing unwavering commitment and daily hard work. Balancing ambition with patience and the importance of perseverance are highlighted, leading to the cultivation of a growth-oriented mindset for sustained success. Readers are invited to embark on a chapter that sets the stage for personal and professional transformation.

3 MASTERING THE ART OF RISK AND READINESS

"Every problem is a puzzle waiting to be solved. In entrepreneurship, navigating financial challenges, adapting to changes, and satisfying customers is the key to unlocking success."

Welcome to a pivotal chapter in your entrepreneurial journey, where we navigate the intricate landscape of risks and unveil the art of preparedness. Like a winding road, entrepreneurship is laden with challenges and opportunities. Join me as we delve into the critical facets of risk management and embrace preparedness, which is indispensable for any entrepreneur.

QUALITIES OF A SUCCESSFUL ENTREPRENEUR:

Becoming a successful entrepreneur requires a unique blend of qualities and skills. Here's an introduction to 12 key attributes that contribute to entrepreneurial success:

- **Products or Services Execution and Market Understanding:**
  Successful entrepreneurs excel in executing, marketing, and selling their products or services. They deeply understand their consumers, the marketplace, and the needs that drive supply and demand.

- **Passion to Succeed:**
  Passion is a driving force for successful entrepreneurs. Genuine enthusiasm and commitment to their ventures fuel the resilience needed to overcome challenges.

- **Strong Work Ethic or Discipline:**
  Entrepreneurs with a strong work ethic exhibit discipline in managing their time, resources, and tasks. This

discipline ensures consistent effort and progress.

- **Determination:**
Determination is the unwavering resolve to achieve goals despite obstacles. Successful entrepreneurs possess a strong sense of determination, allowing them to persevere through setbacks. Have Faith In Your Venture. Believe in yourself.

- **Motivation:**
Motivation is the internal drive that propels entrepreneurs forward. Successful individuals are self-motivated, inspiring themselves and their teams to achieve greatness.

- **Strong Commitment:**
Commitment involves dedicating oneself to the goals and vision of the business. Successful entrepreneurs are deeply committed to their ventures, fostering trust and loyalty.

- **Focus:**
Focus is the ability to concentrate on critical tasks and objectives. Entrepreneurs who maintain focus can navigate challenges and stay on course toward achieving long-term goals.

- **Risk Taker:**
Entrepreneurship involves calculated risk-taking. Successful entrepreneurs are willing to take risks, understanding that strategic risk can lead to innovation and growth.

- **Creative Thinker and Strategic Planner:**
Creativity allows entrepreneurs to think creatively, generating innovative solutions. Coupled with strategic planning, this creativity ensures a thoughtful and forward-looking approach.

- **Emotional Stability:**
Emotional stability is crucial in the face of uncertainty

and stress. Successful entrepreneurs maintain composure, making sound decisions even in challenging situations.

- **Ensure Sufficient Funding for Business Expansion and Growth:**
  Adequate financing plays a crucial role in the scalability of a business. Successful entrepreneurs secure the required funds to elevate operations, establish infrastructure, and propel overall growth. Maintaining a capital reserve is prudent, with a recommended minimum of 6 to 12 months and ideally extending up to 3-plus years. Building a business typically takes 3 to 5 years, and the timeline can vary across industries, be it product-oriented, service-based, or otherwise. Additionally, many entrepreneurs commit to lease agreements, often spanning 3 to 5 years, as required by rental managers or lessors. Once locked into a lease, whether the business performs exceptionally well or faces challenges, rent obligations must be fulfilled throughout the agreed-upon term.

- **Long-Term Planning:**
  Long-term planning involves setting a vision for the future and devising strategies to achieve it. Successful entrepreneurs are adept at long-term planning, aligning actions with overarching goals.

WAYS TO MEASURE ENTREPRENEURS' SUCCESS IN THEIR VENTURE:

Assessing the success of an entrepreneurial venture involves more than just financial metrics; it encompasses a comprehensive evaluation of various aspects that contribute to the business's overall health and impact. Entrepreneurs employ a range of metrics to gauge progress and ensure the sustainability and growth of their ventures. Let's explore key indicators used to measure entrepreneurs' success:

Company Revenue Growth:
A fundamental measure of success is the growth of a company's revenue over time. Increasing revenue reflects the ability of the business to attract customers, deliver value, and capitalize on market opportunities. Sustainable revenue growth is often indicative of a well-performing and competitive venture.

EBITDA (Earnings Before Interest, Taxes, Depreciation, and Amortization):
EBITDA serves as a crucial financial metric to assess a company's profitability. By excluding certain expenses, it provides a clearer picture of the core operational earnings. Entrepreneurs use EBITDA to evaluate the financial health of their venture and make informed decisions regarding investments, expansions, or strategic adjustments.

Market Share and Position:
Entrepreneurs monitor their market share and position relative to competitors. Gaining market share signifies success in attracting customers and outperforming rivals. Evaluating market position helps entrepreneurs identify areas for improvement, innovation, and strategies to enhance their standing within the industry.

Reaching Goals and Milestones:
Establishing specific goals and milestones is crucial in tracking the progress of an entrepreneurial venture. These goals may include product launches, market expansion, customer acquisition targets, or other key performance indicators. Achieving set milestones indicates effective planning and execution, contributing to the overall success of the venture.

Customer and Employee Satisfaction:
Success extends beyond financial metrics to encompass the satisfaction of both customers and employees. High customer satisfaction reflects the quality of products or

services and contributes to customer loyalty and retention. Likewise, a satisfied and engaged workforce is an essential indicator of a well-managed and sustainable business.

CONSIDERING BUSINESS VARIATIONS

Every business, industry, trade, or location has unique challenges and opportunities. Entrepreneurs must carefully analyze and envision how they will operate. This chapter sheds light on understanding variations critical for sustained success.

MOST SUCCESSFUL SMALL BUSINESS IDEAS:

Embarking on a small business venture can be rewarding, especially when considering low-cost, service-oriented opportunities. Here's an introduction to 15 successful small business ideas that require minimal capital investment or startup costs:

- **Arts, Graphic Design, Interior Design, etc.:**
  Creative services such as graphic design, interior design, and other artistic endeavors can be launched with minimal upfront costs, catering to clients seeking visually appealing solutions.

- **Any Service-Related Business, etc.:**
  Exploring various service-related business ideas, from consulting to specialized services, provides entrepreneurs with various possibilities tailored to their skills and interests.

- **Babysitting, Senior Care, Personal Assistant, etc.:**
  Providing personal assistance services, including babysitting, senior care, or acting as a personal assistant, offers a valuable solution for individuals with busy lifestyles or those needing specialized care.

- **Boutique, Salon, Spa, Beauty Salon, Haircut, Facial, etc.:**
  Beauty and wellness services, including boutique shops, salons, spas, and beauty services, cater to individuals seeking personal grooming and relaxation.

- **Computer Training Center, Troubleshooting, Web-Design, Networking, Tech Consulting, etc.:**
  Services related to computer training, troubleshooting, web design, networking, and tech consulting tap into the ever-expanding digital landscape.

- **Cooking, Arts and Craft Classes, etc.:**
  Conducting cooking classes or arts and crafts workshops can be a fulfilling business idea, tapping into people's interests and hobbies.

- **Driving School, Cab Service, Uber, Delivery Service, etc.:**
  Ventures related to transportation, such as driving schools, cab services, or delivery services, cater to the mobility needs of individuals and businesses.

- **Executive Assistant, Secretary, etc.:**
  Offering administrative support services to businesses, entrepreneurs, or executives can be a lucrative venture with minimal startup expenses.

- **Event, Wedding Planner, Photography, Video Editing Services, etc.:**
  Event planning, wedding coordination, and photography/videography services capitalize on the demand for capturing and celebrating life's special moments.

- **Food Catering Business, Home Base Cooking, etc.:**
  Starting a food catering business or offering home-based cooking services leverages the popularity of culinary experiences and the convenience of delivered meals.

- **Fitness Centers, Personal Coaches, etc.:**
  Establishing a fitness center or providing personal coaching services meets the growing demand for health and wellness solutions.

- **Gutter Cleanup/Painting, etc.:**
  Offering specialized services like gutter cleanup or painting addresses specific needs in property maintenance.

- **Landscaping, Handyman, Cleanup Services, etc.:**
  Home improvement and maintenance services, such as landscaping, handyman work, or cleanup services, address the growing demand for property enhancement.

- **Pet Care and Grooming, etc.:**
  Establishing a pet care and grooming service caters to pet owners looking for reliable and caring services for their furry friends.

- **Tuition/Coaching Classes, Other Subjects, etc.:**
  Providing tutoring or coaching services in various subjects meets the educational needs of students, offering personalized learning experiences.

THINGS TO CONSIDER BEFORE TAKING THE PLUNGE

Embarking on the entrepreneurial journey is a monumental decision; thorough preparation is the key to success. Drawing from my own experiences, we explore essential considerations before taking the plunge:

1. **Personal and Financial Readiness:**
   Entrepreneurship's emotional and financial aspects cannot be overstated. Assess your personal and financial stability before leaping into the demanding world of entrepreneurship.

2. **Market Analysis:**
   Understanding the market dynamics is crucial in creating a roadmap for your business. I share insights into effective market research, helping you identify lucrative niches and understand your competition.

3. **Support System:**
   The journey is fraught with challenges, and a robust support system is your anchor. Learn from my experiences how the unwavering support of family, friends, and mentors played a pivotal role in my entrepreneurial success.

4. **Competitive Advantage:**
   Setting yourself apart is a cornerstone of entrepreneurship. Discover the importance of creating a Unique Selling Proposition (USP) and how it can be a powerful differentiator in a competitive landscape.

5. **Personal Fulfillment:**
   Aligning your business with your passions is the key to long-term success. Explore the significance of pursuing a company that genuinely interests and fulfills you.

BACKUP PLANS AND EXIT STRATEGIES

Entrepreneurship demands foresight and resilience. This section dives into the art of preparedness with a focus on backup plans and exit strategies:

1. **Contingency Planning:**
   Acquire the skills to establish vital support systems for your business with proficient contingency planning. Drawing from my experiences, I gain practical perspectives on crafting resilient backup strategies to address unforeseen challenges. Ensure thorough planning, establish contingency measures, prepare for worst-case scenarios, and prioritize safety over regrets. In the unpredictable business realm, cautiousness is valuable, especially when uncertainties surround aspects

such as breaking even, turning a profit, or building success over time.

2. **Pivoting and Adaptability:**
   Flexibility is paramount in entrepreneurship. My journey underscores the importance of adaptability and making necessary changes to your business plans as circumstances evolve.

3. **Mitigating Risks:**
   Reducing potential risks is a crucial part of entrepreneurial preparedness. Explore actionable strategies to mitigate risks and safeguard your venture from unforeseen obstacles.

4. **Exit Strategies:**
   Not all businesses last forever, and having a clear exit strategy is essential. This section explores various exit strategies, including selling your business, passing it down to family, or gracefully closing it if necessary.

Chapter Summary

Chapter 3 is your comprehensive guide to mastering the art of risk and readiness. Whether you're an aspiring entrepreneur or an established business owner, this chapter equips you with the knowledge, strategies, and mindset needed to navigate challenges, prepare for unexpected events, and maintain unwavering determination on your path to success. Embrace the adventure of entrepreneurship, let perseverance be your guiding light, and fortify your journey with the readiness to manage risks effectively. Your ability to navigate uncertainties will define the trajectory of your entrepreneurial success. Welcome to a chapter that empowers you for the challenges and rewards that lie ahead.

4 NAVIGATING THE SEAS OF ENTREPRENEURIAL CHALLENGES

"Resilience is the secret weapon of every successful entrepreneur. In the face of trials, triumphs emerge, turning stories of struggle into narratives of extraordinary success."

Join me as we embark on a voyage through the intricate waters of problem-solving in entrepreneurship. In this chapter, we'll uncover the hurdles and explore actionable strategies for managing finances, securing investments, and ensuring the financial stability of your business. The journey may seem daunting but fear not—with the right approach, you can steer your entrepreneurial ship through turbulent waters and emerge stronger on the other side.

FINANCIAL MASTERY:

SAILING THROUGH THE SEA OF BUDGETS AND INVESTMENTS

- **Budgeting Mastery:**
  Embark on the journey of financial control by developing a comprehensive budget outlining your business's income and expenses. Regularly review and adjust it to navigate the seas of economic fluctuations confidently.

- **Money as a Tool:**
  Viewing money as a tool emphasizes its role in achieving financial goals. A master budget harnesses the power of money as a strategic resource to allocate, invest, and fulfill both short-term and long-term objectives.

- **Document Your Transactions:**
  Documenting transactions involves meticulous record-keeping of all financial activities. This step is crucial for maintaining transparency, understanding cash flows, and ensuring accuracy in budgetary planning.

- **Monitor Your Spending:**
  Regular monitoring of spending habits allows for a real-time assessment of financial health. This helps identify areas where adjustments may be needed and provides insights into maintaining a balanced budget.

- **Make a Budget:**
  Creating a budget involves outlining income, expenses, and savings goals. A well-structured budget serves as a roadmap, guiding financial decisions and promoting disciplined financial behavior.

- **Write Everything Down:**
  Writing down financial details reinforces accountability and promotes a clear understanding of the budget. Tangible documentation allows for easy reference and analysis, aiding in informed decision-making.

- **Plan Ahead:**
  Planning involves anticipating and incorporating future financial needs into the budget. This proactive approach helps individuals or businesses prepare for upcoming expenses and navigate financial challenges more effectively.

- **Make a Program Work for You:**
  Utilizing budgeting tools or software programs tailored to individual or organizational needs enhances efficiency and accuracy. Customized programs can automate certain processes, making it easier to manage and adhere to the master budget.

- **Financial Forecasting:**
  Anticipate the tides of future financial trends through

effective forecasting. This proactive approach lets you make informed decisions, ensuring your ship sails smoothly even in changing financial landscapes.

- **Investment Exploration:**
  Explore diverse avenues for securing investments, from venture capital to angel investors and crowdfunding platforms tailored to your business. Discover the keys to unlocking financial support and fueling the growth of your entrepreneurial vessel.

- **Diversification Strategies:**
  Minimize the impact of financial challenges by diversifying your revenue streams. Explore complementary services or products that align with your business model, ensuring your ship remains resilient amid economic storms.

ESSENTIAL INSURANCE FOR YOUR SAILING ADVENTURE:

Just like any good captain charts a course and prepares for rough seas, smart entrepreneurs safeguard their business with insurance. Here are some key policies to consider:

Protecting Your Ship and Crew:
- **General Liability Insurance:**
  General Liability Insurance: This acts as your first mate, covering accidental injuries or liability damage caused by your business activities. Think of it as a safety net for everyday mishaps.

- **Business Owner's Policy (BOP):**
  This comprehensive package combines general liability with coverage for your business property (including the building, if owned). It's a one-stop shop for essential protection.

Navigating the Workforce Waters:

- **Workers' Compensation:**
  Mandatory if you have employees, this covers work-related injuries and illnesses. Consider it a lifeline for your team in case of unexpected accidents.

- **Errors & Omissions (E&O) or Professional Liability:**
  For professionals like lawyers or consultants, this protects against claims of negligence. Think of it as a compass guiding you through ethical practice.

Weathering Unexpected Storms:

- **Commercial Flood & Earthquake Insurance:**
  These specialized policies help you stay afloat in the face of natural disasters. Remember, it's better to be prepared than caught off guard.

- **Cyber Insurance:**
  In today's digital world, this is your shield against cyber-attacks and data breaches. It's essential for any business relying on technology.

Investing in Smooth Sailing:

- **Directors & Officers Insurance (D&O):**
  This protects your company's leaders from personal liability in certain situations. Think of it as a sturdy hull protecting your captains.

- **Employment Practices Liability Insurance (EPLI):**
  Mitigate legal risks associated with employee issues like discrimination or wrongful termination. This acts as an anchor for smooth employee relations.

- **Employee Benefits:**
  Offering health, dental, vision **life insurance, and retirement planning/annuity attracts** and retains talented crew members. It's an investment in your team's well-being and your future success.

  Note: Business insurance is usually tax-deductible. Consult a financial advisor to explore specific options and tailor your coverage to your unique needs.

By proactively integrating these insurance considerations, you can confidently navigate the entrepreneurial seas, weathering inevitable storms and charting a course towards long-term success. Bon voyage!

<u>WINDS OF CHANGE:</u>
NAVIGATING COMPETITION AND MARKET SHIFTS

In the dynamic sea of the business world, market conditions can change as swiftly as the wind. Explore how to adapt to fierce competition and navigate the unpredictable currents of market fluctuations.

Continuous Market Research:
Stay ahead of the tide by regularly conducting market research. Understand industry trends, competitor strategies, and changing consumer preferences to set sail with a strategic advantage.

Market Research Categories:
- **Primary Market:**
  The primary market refers to collecting original data directly from sources, such as potential customers, through methods like surveys, interviews, or observations. This firsthand information is specific to the research objectives and tailored to the study's unique needs.

- **Secondary Market:**
  In contrast, the secondary market involves analyzing and utilizing existing data. This data is not collected firsthand but is sourced from various published materials, industry reports, or previously conducted research. Secondary market research provides valuable context and background information.

- **Quantitative Research:**
  Quantitative research involves collecting and analyzing numerical data to quantify patterns, trends, and statistical relationships. It uses structured surveys, experiments, or statistical modeling to derive measurable insights. This method is useful for assessing market size, demographics, and numerical trends.

- **Qualitative Research:**
  Qualitative research gathers non-numerical data to explore attitudes, opinions, and in-depth insights. Methods such as interviews, focus groups, and customer observations are common in qualitative research. This approach provides a nuanced understanding of consumer behavior, preferences, and motivations.

Four Types of Market Research:
a) **Surveys:**
  Surveys involve the systematic collection of data through structured questionnaires, either online, via phone, or in person. They effectively gather quantitative data on consumer preferences, satisfaction, and demographics.

b) **Interviews:**
  Interviews allow for in-depth conversations between researchers and participants. This qualitative method is valuable for exploring complex opinions, perceptions, and experiences. Interviews provide a deeper understanding of individual perspectives.

c) **Focus Groups:**
  Focus groups bring together a small, diverse group of participants to discuss and provide feedback on a specific product, service, or idea. This qualitative method facilitates interactive discussions, uncovering collective attitudes and perceptions.

d) Customer Observation:

Customer observation involves directly observing and documenting consumer behavior in natural settings. This method provides real-time insights into how customers interact with products or services, helping to identify pain points and areas for improvement.

Agile Business Models:

Foster agility in your business model, being prepared to pivot when necessary. Embrace change as an opportunity for growth rather than a threat, and navigate the unpredictable winds of market dynamics with finesse.

Customer Feedback Loops:

Establish feedback loops with your customers to understand their evolving needs and expectations. Use this insight to tailor your offerings and stay ahead of the competition, ensuring your ship remains on course.

Strategic Partnerships:

Explore collaboration opportunities with complementary businesses. Strategic partnerships can enhance your market position and provide resilience against market uncertainties, creating a stronger vessel for your entrepreneurial journey.

Identify Goals and Value Proposition:

Before pursuing a strategic partnership, it's crucial to identify your business goals and what value each partner brings to the table. Understanding the mutual benefits and aligning goals helps create a foundation for a successful collaboration.

Set Expectations:

Clearly defining expectations from the outset is vital for a healthy and productive partnership. This involves communicating roles, responsibilities, and anticipated outcomes. A transparent discussion about expectations helps prevent misunderstandings later on.

Decide Your Partnership:
Assess potential partners based on their compatibility with your goals, industry reputation, and the specific expertise or resources they can contribute. Choose partners whose strengths complement your weaknesses, creating a synergy that enhances overall capabilities.

Make an Agreement:
Formalizing the terms and conditions of the partnership through a well-structured agreement is essential. This document should outline the scope of collaboration, responsibilities, expectations, and any financial arrangements. Legal guidance may be advisable during this process

Pair Up with a Partner with a Good Brand, Business Model, or Operations:
Selecting a partner with a strong brand, sound business model, or efficient operations enhances the likelihood of a successful collaboration. A partner with a positive reputation can contribute to the partnership's credibility and positively impact both entities' perceptions.

NAVIGATING DAILY INTRICACIES:

OPERATIONAL MASTERY

Running a business involves a myriad of operational tasks, each presenting its unique set of challenges. Walk with me through the day-to-day intricacies of entrepreneurship as we uncover valuable lessons on optimizing operations, improving efficiency, and overcoming obstacles.

- **Process Optimization:**
  Streamline your business processes to enhance efficiency. Identify bottlenecks and implement improvements to ensure smooth day-to-day operations, allowing your ship to navigate the intricate currents easily.

- **Technology Integration:**
  Explore technology solutions that can automate repetitive tasks and improve operational efficiency. Embrace digital tools that align with your business needs, steering your ship toward technological excellence.

- **Employee Training and Empowerment:**
  Invest in the training and empowerment of your team. An educated and motivated workforce contributes significantly to overcoming operational challenges, making your ship resilient in the face of daily intricacies.

- **Evaluate Training Needs:**
  Before implementing any training program, it's essential to assess employees' specific needs. This evaluation helps identify skills, knowledge, or performance gaps, allowing for targeted and effective training initiatives.

- **Learning Objectives:**
  Clearly defined learning objectives set the foundation for a successful training program. These objectives outline what employees are expected to achieve, providing a roadmap for the training content and assessments.

- **Apply Different Training Styles:**
  People learn in diverse ways, and incorporating various training styles accommodates different learning preferences. This might include hands-on activities, workshops, online modules, or mentorship programs, ensuring a more inclusive and effective training experience.

- **Put Together Training Materials:**
  Developing comprehensive and engaging training materials is key to effective learning. These materials may include presentations, manuals, interactive modules, and other resources that support the learning objectives.

- **Evaluate Progress:**
  Regularly assessing and evaluating employees' progress during and after training is crucial. This feedback loop allows adjustments to the training program, ensuring it remains relevant, impactful, and aligned with organizational goals.

- **Build Knowledge and Skill:**
  Training should address immediate needs and contribute to employees' long-term growth. Building both knowledge and skills ensures that individuals are equipped to handle current responsibilities and are prepared for future challenges.

- **Increase Output and Efficiency:**
  The ultimate goal of employee training and empowerment is to enhance overall output and efficiency. Organizations can expect improved performance, increased productivity, and a more skilled workforce by providing employees with the necessary tools and knowledge.

- **Continuous Improvement Culture:**
  Foster a culture of continuous improvement within your organization. Encourage employees to identify areas for improvement and implement changes collaboratively, ensuring your ship sails towards operational excellence.

MASTERING THE ART OF CUSTOMER SATISFACTION

At the heart of any successful venture lies customer satisfaction. Discover how to prioritize excellent customer service and build strong, lasting relationships with clients.

- **Personalized Customer Experiences:**
  Tailor your products or services to meet your customers' unique needs and preferences. Personalization enhances customer satisfaction and fosters loyalty, making your

ship a preferred choice on the seas of consumer options.

- **Effective Communication Channels:**
Establish clear and effective communication channels with your customers. Be responsive to inquiries, feedback, and concerns to build trust and satisfaction, ensuring your ship sails on the seas of customer relations with ease.

- **Customer Loyalty Programs:**
Implement loyalty programs to reward repeat customers. Incentivize loyalty through exclusive discounts, promotions, or personalized offerings, anchoring your ship in the hearts of your clientele.

- **Proactive Issue Resolution:**
Anticipate potential issues and proactively address them. Swift and effective issue resolution demonstrates your commitment to customer satisfaction and builds trust, guiding your ship through the challenging waters of customer relations.

By implementing these ideas, you learn from my experiences and actively apply strategies that can make a tangible difference in your entrepreneurial journey. Remember, each challenge is an opportunity for growth, and your proactive approach can transform obstacles into stepping stones toward lasting success. Welcome to a chapter that equips you with the tools to navigate the seas of entrepreneurial challenges with resilience and mastery.

STEPS TO SUCCESS:

Achieving success in any endeavor requires a strategic approach and a steadfast commitment to certain principles. The path to success is often marked by specific steps that, when diligently followed, can pave the way for significant accomplishments. Let's explore the fundamental elements encapsulated in the "6 Steps to Success" and understand how they contribute to the journey of achieving one's goals:

1. **Set a Clear Goal:**
    The first step toward success involves setting a clear and well-defined goal. This establishes a purpose and direction for your efforts. Clear goals serve as a roadmap, guiding your actions and decisions throughout the journey. Whether in business, personal development, or any other pursuit, a defined objective provides focus and motivation.

2. **Make a Good Plan:**
    Success is often the result of meticulous planning. Creating a comprehensive and well-thought-out plan involves outlining the steps, resources, and timelines required to reach your goal. A strategic plan serves as a blueprint, helping you navigate challenges and capitalize on opportunities while maintaining a structured approach to your endeavors.

3. **Stay Focused and Committed:**
    The journey to success demands unwavering focus and commitment. Distractions and setbacks are inevitable, but successful individuals remain steadfast in their pursuit. Maintaining focus involves prioritizing tasks, managing time effectively, and staying committed to the objectives outlined in the plan, even when faced with challenges.

4. **Work Very Hard:**
    Hard work is a cornerstone of success. Diligence, perseverance, and a strong work ethic contribute to the attainment of goals. Success rarely comes without effort, and consistently putting in the work is essential to overcoming obstacles, honing skills, and making meaningful progress toward your desired outcomes.

5. **Stay Humble:**
    Humility plays a vital role in the journey to success. Acknowledging that there is always room for improvement, remaining open to learning from others,

and embracing a humble mindset fosters personal and professional growth. Humility also contributes to building positive relationships and collaborative endeavors, enhancing the overall journey toward success.

6. **Don't Give Up:**
Resilience is a key attribute of successful individuals. The path to success is rarely linear, and setbacks are inevitable. The ability to persevere in the face of challenges, learn from failures, and keep moving forward is what sets successful individuals apart. Choosing not to give up, even when the journey becomes arduous, is a defining characteristic of those who ultimately achieve their goals.

GREATEST SECRET TO ENTREPRENEURIAL SUCCESS:

Secrets to Become a Successful Entrepreneur

The journey to entrepreneurial success is paved with strategic principles and essential practices. Here are the 8 greatest secrets that aspiring entrepreneurs can leverage to unlock their full potential and achieve lasting success:

1. **Well Defined Business Operations/ Organization is Key:**
A solid foundation begins with a clear and well-defined structure for your business operations and organization. This includes establishing efficient processes, defining roles, and implementing systems that foster smooth functioning.

2. **Never Stop Learning to Acquire More Knowledge:**
Pursuing knowledge is a continuous journey. Successful entrepreneurs prioritize ongoing learning, staying abreast of industry trends, emerging technologies, and evolving market dynamics to make informed decisions and adapt

to change.

3. **Flexibility/Adaptability:**
   Flexibility and adaptability are indispensable traits. Entrepreneurs must navigate a dynamic landscape, adjusting their strategies to respond to market shifts, emerging opportunities, and unforeseen challenges.

4. **Do Not Be Afraid to Ask for Help:**
   Entrepreneurial success often involves collaboration and seeking guidance. Smart entrepreneurs are not afraid to ask for help, leveraging the expertise of mentors, advisors, and industry peers to gain insights and overcome obstacles.

5. **Develop a Well-Rounded and Supportive Team:**
   Building a strong and supportive team is a cornerstone of success. Entrepreneurs should focus on assembling a diverse group of individuals with complementary skills, fostering a collaborative environment that encourages innovation and growth.

6. **Know Your Customers and Market Well:**
   In-depth knowledge of the target market and understanding customer needs is fundamental. Successful entrepreneurs invest time in market research, customer feedback, and analytics to tailor their products or services to meet the demands of their audience.

7. **Think Out-of-the-Box (Creative, Innovative, and Unconventional):**
   Creative thinking and innovation set successful entrepreneurs apart. Thinking beyond conventional boundaries, exploring unique solutions, and embracing innovation can lead to breakthroughs and a competitive edge in the market.

8. **Invest in Risk Management Strategy, Implementation, and Operations:**
   Entrepreneurship inherently involves risks, but strategic risk management is a key component of long-term

success. Entrepreneurs should invest in robust risk management strategies, implementing measures to mitigate potential pitfalls and ensure operational resilience.

15 D's OF ENTREPRENEURSHIP:

The 15 Ds of Entrepreneurship encapsulate the essential qualities and actions that contribute to the success of individuals venturing into the world of business. Each "D" represents a critical aspect entrepreneur should cultivate and integrate into their entrepreneurial journey. Here's a brief introduction to each of the 15 Ds:

1. **Dream:** Start with a vision or dream that inspires you. What do you want to achieve with your business?

2. **Determination:** Entrepreneurship requires perseverance and determination. Be ready to overcome challenges and setbacks.

3. **Dedication:** Commit to your goals and stay dedicated to your business. Success often requires hard work and sacrifice.

4. **Drive:** Have the inner motivation and ambition to advance your business.

5. **Decision-Making:** Effective decision-making is crucial. Entrepreneurs need to make sound and timely decisions for their business to succeed.

6. **Design Thinking:** Apply creative and innovative thinking to design products or services that meet the needs of your target market.

7. **Differentiation:** Stand out from the competition by offering unique value. Differentiate your products or services in the marketplace.

8. **Deliver Value:**
Focus on delivering value to your customers. A successful business often revolves around meeting customer needs and exceeding their expectations.

9. **Dynamic Adaptability:**
Be adaptable to change and adjust your strategies based on market trends and feedback.

10. **Delegation:**
Learn to delegate tasks effectively. As your business grows, you can't do everything on your own.

11. **Development:**
Continuously invest in personal and professional development. Stay updated on industry trends and improve your skills.

12. **Diversification:**
Consider diversifying your products, services, or markets to minimize risk and explore new opportunities.

13. **Documentation:**
Keep proper records and documentation. This is crucial for compliance, financial management, and strategic planning.

14. **Discipline:**
Develop a disciplined approach to managing your time, resources, and business operations.

15. **Digital Presence:**
A strong digital presence is essential in the modern business landscape. Leverage digital tools and platforms to reach a wider audience.

These 15 Ds collectively form a comprehensive framework for aspiring and established entrepreneurs, guiding them toward realizing their visions and building successful ventures.

5 TALES OF TRIUMPH AND UNYIELDING RESILIENCE

"Your business vision is not just a goal; it's the North Star guiding your entrepreneurial expedition. Craft it meticulously, and watch it illuminate your path to success."

Embark on an enriching chapter as we delve into the profound narratives of entrepreneurs who traversed the unpredictable landscape of business, overcoming adversities with remarkable resilience. In this exploration, our focus zooms in on the distinctive challenge's minority entrepreneurs face, drawing profound inspiration from their extraordinary journey.

UNIQUE CHALLENGES OF MINORITY ENTREPRENEURS

Diversity in Entrepreneurship:
Delve into the profound significance of diversity in the entrepreneurial landscape. Explore the invaluable perspectives minority entrepreneurs bring to the business table, enriching the entire entrepreneurial ecosystem.

Overcoming Barriers:
Understand the specific hurdles that minority entrepreneurs confront, from limited access to funding and discrimination to cultural biases. Explore the diverse strategies employed to overcome these challenges, carving out unique paths to success.

Success Against the Odds:
Uncover compelling stories of minority entrepreneurs who defied barriers, achieving remarkable success. These narratives underscore the potent blend of resilience and determination in overcoming adversity and achieving extraordinary feats.

OVERCOMING HURDLES:

UNVEILING ENTREPRENEURS' REALITIES

Trials and Tribulations:
Entrepreneurship, akin to a rollercoaster, invites us into the authentic experiences of those who navigated its twists and turns. Immerse yourself in firsthand accounts of entrepreneurs confronting adversity. Their narratives traverse financial struggles, intense competition, and personal setbacks, vividly depicting the diverse challenges one might encounter and the strategic maneuvers that led to triumph.

Personal Insight: The Insurance Industry Saga:
In the insurance realm, entering an already saturated market posed substantial challenges. Despite skepticism, my insurance journey underscored the power of confidence and hard work. Learning from industry peers, keenly observing, and understanding the intricacies became my strategies. With belief, dedication, and a well-thought-out plan, success became achievable and inevitable.

Turning Points:
Explore pivotal moments where entrepreneurs made critical decisions that redirected the course of their businesses toward success. Unravel the intricate dance between challenges and strategic choices, understanding how these turning points shaped their trajectories.

Inspirational Success:
Uncover the transformative power of resilience and determination that elevated these entrepreneurs from ordinary individuals to extraordinary success stories. Their journeys serve as beacons of inspiration for anyone navigating the unpredictable terrain of entrepreneurship.

DRAWING INSPIRATION FROM RESILIENT ENTREPRENEURS

Resilience as a Virtue:
Explore the defining characteristics of resilient entrepreneurs—adaptability, a growth mindset, and the unwavering ability to persevere in the face of setbacks. Understand how these virtues form the bedrock of their journey.

Applying Resilience in Your Journey:
Discover actionable insights on applying the principles of resilience to your entrepreneurial path. These lessons empower you to navigate challenges with finesse, turning each obstacle into a stepping stone for personal and business growth.

Chapter Summary

Chapter 5 extends a heartfelt invitation to explore entrepreneurs' triumphs and unyielding resilience. Whether facing common challenges or encountering unique hurdles as a minority entrepreneur, this chapter serves as a rich source of inspiration and strength. As a cultivated quality, resilience proves to be an invaluable asset in overcoming the most formidable obstacles. These real-life stories provide motivation and practical guidance, fostering unwavering determination as you navigate the challenges of your entrepreneurial journey.

6 NURTURING YOUR ENTREPRENEURIAL VISION

"No entrepreneur thrives in isolation. Building a supportive network is not just about collaboration; it's about creating a foundation for collaborative success that withstands the test of challenges."

In Chapter 6, we embark on a pivotal exploration, delving into the craftsmanship of your business vision. This vision is not merely a goal; the North Star guides your entrepreneurial expedition. Throughout this chapter, we'll unravel the steps to cultivate a comprehensive business plan, understand the importance of meticulous market research, and learn how to keep the flame of success burning, illuminating your path at every step.

CORE PILLARS OF BUSINESS

Building a resilient and thriving venture requires a solid foundation in the dynamic landscape of entrepreneurship. The success of your business hinges on the careful development and management of five essential pillars. These pillars collectively form the bedrock upon which your entrepreneurial journey rests.

1. **People:** The first pillar centers on the human element—the individuals who drive, support, and contribute to your venture. From skilled employees to effective leadership, creating a cohesive and talented team is paramount. People are the heart of your business, influencing its culture, productivity, and overall success.

2. **Product:** At the core of your enterprise is the product or service you offer. This pillar emphasizes the importance of crafting a compelling and valuable offering that meets

the needs of your target market. A well-defined and innovative product sets the stage for differentiation, customer satisfaction, and market competitiveness.

3. **Process:** Efficient and streamlined processes form the third pillar, ensuring the smooth operation of your business. From internal workflows to customer interactions, well-designed processes enhance productivity, reduce costs, and contribute to a positive customer experience. This pillar focuses on the optimization of operations for sustained success.

4. **Profit:** The pillar of profit is essential to any venture's sustainability. Financial viability is a key consideration, encompassing revenue generation, cost management, and profitability. A robust financial strategy is vital for weathering challenges, fostering growth, and achieving long-term success.

5. **Permanence:** The fifth pillar, permanence, underscores the importance of long-term thinking and strategic planning. Building a business that withstands the test of time requires foresight, adaptability, and a commitment to lasting impact. This pillar encourages entrepreneurs to consider their ventures' enduring legacy and continuity.

These five core pillars collectively form the strategic framework for entrepreneurs to navigate challenges, seize opportunities, and establish a resilient business venture. Each pillar contributes a crucial element to the overall success and sustainability of the entrepreneurial journey.

<u>FROM VISION TO REALITY:</u>

BLUEPRINTING YOUR BUSINESS PLAN

The Power of a Clear Vision: Immerse yourself into a business vision—a potent roadmap for your entrepreneurial journey. Learn the art of envisioning your business's future and setting precise, measurable goals as the cornerstone of your strategic direction.

- **Constructing a Business Plan:**
  Delve into the intricate components of a well-structured business plan. From defining your mission statement and business objectives to crafting a detailed action plan, understand the pivotal role of timelines and milestones in charting your progress.

- **Executive Summary:**
  The executive summary is a concise overview of the business plan, highlighting key elements such as the business concept, mission, goals, and a snapshot of financial projections. Despite being the first section, it is often written last, summarizing the plan's main points.

- **Company Description:**
  This section provides detailed information about the business, including its mission, vision, values, legal structure, location, and history. It sets the stage for understanding the company's identity and purpose.

- **Products and Services:**
  Here, businesses outline their products or services, emphasizing unique selling points and value propositions. It details features, benefits, and how offerings meet customer needs.

- **Market Analysis:**
  Conducting a thorough analysis of the market is essential. This includes assessing the industry landscape, target market demographics, competition, and market trends. The goal is to demonstrate a deep understanding of the business's environment.

- **Marketing Strategy:**
  The marketing strategy outlines how the business plans to reach and attract its target audience. This section includes the marketing mix (product, price, place, promotion) and details promotional tactics, distribution

channels, and sales strategies.

- **Financials:**
  Financial projections, including income statements, balance sheets, and cash flow statements, are critical components. This section provides a snapshot of the business's financial health and viability, often projecting three to five years into the future.

- **Budget:**
  The budget section breaks down expected costs and revenues, helping to manage financial resources effectively. It includes startup costs, operational expenses, and revenue projections, contributing to a realistic and actionable financial plan.

- **Mapping Out Your Strategy:**
  Develop a strategic plan outlining the steps to morph your vision into a flourishing business. This encompasses product or service development, marketing, sales, and operational efficiency considerations.

THE ROLE OF MARKET RESEARCH

1. **Understanding Your Target Market:**
   Uncover the critical role of market research in sculpting your business vision. Learn the art of identifying your target audience, deciphering their needs, and foreseeing market trends.

2. **Competition Analysis:**
   Grasp the significance of assessing your competitors. Gain insights into competitive analysis, a tool shaping your unique selling points and refining your business strategy.

3. **Adapting to Market Changes:**
   Recognize that market research is not a one-time endeavor but an ongoing necessity. Explore strategies to

remain agile and responsive to industry and consumer behavior shifts.

A BURNING DESIRE FOR SUCCESS:

IGNITING YOUR VISION

1. **Maintaining Your Drive:**
   Entrepreneurship is a prolonged and often challenging expedition. Discover strategies for sustaining enthusiasm and determination, even when faced with setbacks.

2. **The Power of Passion:**
   Explore the vital role of passion in fueling your vision. Understand how pursuing what you love can be a wellspring of resilience and creativity.

3. **Seeking Inspiration:**
   Unearth techniques to stay motivated and inspired. To fuel your entrepreneurial journey, draw inspiration from diverse sources, including mentors, literature, and success stories.

CRAFTING YOUR BUSINESS VISION

Passion as a Driving Force:
Choose a path aligned with your passion. For instance, my decision to enter the insurance industry stems from a passion for working in a controlled indoor setting—whether at home, the office, or a similar environment. Recognize the importance of enjoying and being comfortable with your work, passionately embracing it, excelling at it, and repeatedly engaging in it without reservation. Furthermore, leverage your ability to design, innovate, or customize your work, setting you apart from others.

Chapter Summary

Chapter 6 serves as the compass for crafting your business vision, laying the foundation for entrepreneurial triumph. It underscores the significance of creating a robust business plan, undertaking effective market research, and nurturing an unyielding desire for success. Your vision forms the core of your enterprise, and this chapter equips you with the knowledge and insights essential to transmute that vision into a thriving reality. By comprehending the pivotal role of these elements, you'll be adept at forging a strategic plan, propelling you toward sustained success and fulfillment on your entrepreneurial journey.

7 CULTIVATING YOUR ENTREPRENEURIAL TRIBE

"Mastering sales and marketing are not just about attracting customers; it's an art that turns your business into a symphony, captivating your audience and ensuring enduring success."

In Chapter 7, we immerse ourselves in a pivotal facet of entrepreneurial success—building your support network. No entrepreneur thrives in isolation, and this chapter serves as your guide to constructing a robust foundation of support. We'll explore the art of assembling a capable team, fostering relationships with partners and vendors, and infusing your determination into the fabric of these connections.

TRAITS FOR CULTIVATING YOUR ENTREPRENEURIAL SPIRIT:

Embarking on the entrepreneurial journey requires unique traits that form the bedrock of success. These 15 traits encapsulate the qualities essential for cultivating an entrepreneurial spirit and laying the groundwork for achievement. Here's a brief introduction to each trait:

1. **Resilience:**
   Resilience is the ability to bounce back from setbacks. Entrepreneurs navigate challenges with resilience, using adversity as a catalyst for growth.

2. **Perseverance:**
   Perseverance involves steadfast persistence in the face of difficulties. Entrepreneurs continue to pursue their goals, undeterred by obstacles.

3. **Innovative/Creative Thinking:**
   Entrepreneurs thrive on innovative and creative thinking. They approach problems with fresh perspectives, finding unique solutions that set them apart.

4. **Risk Tolerance:**
   Risk tolerance is the willingness to take calculated risks. Entrepreneurs embrace uncertainty, recognizing that risk is inherent in pursuing success.

5. **Proactiveness:**
   Proactiveness entails taking initiative. Entrepreneurs don't wait for opportunities; they create them by actively seeking solutions and staying ahead of challenges.

6. **Mission:**
   A clear mission provides purpose. Entrepreneurs define their mission, outlining the fundamental reason for their venture's existence.

7. **Vision:**
   Vision involves a forward-looking perspective. Entrepreneurs envision their desired future, guiding their decisions and actions.

8. **Objective/Goal:**
   Objectives and goals provide direction. Entrepreneurs set specific and achievable objectives, outlining the milestones that lead to their ultimate goals.

9. **Flexibility:**
   Flexibility is the ability to adapt to change. Entrepreneurs remain flexible, adjusting their strategies to align with evolving circumstances.

10. **Persistence:**
    Persistence is the continuous effort toward a goal. Entrepreneurs stay the course, persisting in the pursuit of success despite challenges.

11. Discipline:
Discipline involves self-control and focus. Entrepreneurs cultivate discipline to maintain consistency and stay on track toward their objectives.

12. Determination:
Determination is the unwavering commitment to success. Entrepreneurs approach challenges with determination, ensuring they overcome obstacles.

13. Consistency:
Consistency is key to building credibility. Entrepreneurs maintain consistent effort and performance, earning trust and reliability.

14. Commitment:
Commitment is a deep dedication to one's goals. Entrepreneurs demonstrate commitment by investing time, effort, and resources into their ventures.

15. End Result:
Entrepreneurs keep the result in focus. They clearly understand the outcomes they aim to achieve, guiding every decision and action.

BUILDING A DYNAMIC TEAM:

YOUR ENTREPRENEURIAL BACKBONE

- **The Power of Teamwork:**
  Acknowledge that the entrepreneurial journey is a collective effort. We'll unravel the importance of curating a team of skilled individuals who not only resonate with your vision but also contribute to the execution of your business plan.

- **Separate Workload:**
  Teamwork involves distributing tasks among team members based on their strengths and expertise. This allows for the efficient allocation of responsibilities, ensuring each team member contributes to the project's

success.

- **Share Strengths and Expertise:**
  Team members bring diverse strengths and expertise to the table. By sharing these qualities, teams can overcome challenges more effectively, capitalize on individual talents, and create a well-rounded approach to problem-solving.

- **Complete Tasks and Projects:**
  Teamwork enables the collective completion of tasks and projects. By leveraging the skills and knowledge of each team member, projects can be tackled comprehensively, leading to a more thorough and successful outcome.

- **Leads to Higher Productivity, Fast Completion, and Better Results:**
  The synergy of teamwork often results in higher productivity levels. Collaborative efforts and shared goals contribute to faster project completion and better results. Team members can pool their resources, ideas, and efforts to enhance efficiency.

- **When Working Together, Get Things Done More:**
  Working together fosters a sense of shared responsibility and accountability. A team's collective motivation and support lead to increased initiative and a greater likelihood of accomplishing tasks and objectives.

- **Recruitment and Hiring:**
  Navigate the process of finding, recruiting, and hiring qualified team members and align culturally with your business ethos.

- **Job Planning:**
  Job planning involves defining a vacant position's role, responsibilities, and qualifications. Employers outline the skills, experience, and attributes necessary for success in the role, providing a clear foundation for the

recruitment process.

- **Candidate Sourcing:**
  Candidate sourcing involves actively identifying and attracting potential candidates for a job. This can include strategies such as posting job listings, leveraging social media, utilizing professional networks, and collaborating with recruitment agencies. The goal is to generate a diverse pool of qualified applicants.

- **Screening and Selection Process:**
  The screening and selection process involves reviewing applications, resumes, and cover letters to shortlist candidates who meet the initial criteria. This phase also includes pre-screening assessments to evaluate skills and qualifications, ensuring that only the most suitable candidates progress to the next stages.

- **Interviewing:**
  The interview stage is a critical element in evaluating candidates. It allows employers to assess candidates' qualifications, interpersonal skills, and cultural fit within the organization. Various interview formats, such as behavioral interviews or technical assessments, may be employed to understand a candidate's capabilities comprehensively.

- **Hiring:**
  The final stage involves extending a job offer to the selected candidate. This includes negotiating terms, discussing benefits, and finalizing contractual details. Successful hiring aligns the candidate's aspirations with the organization's goals, fostering a positive and productive employment relationship.

- **Team Dynamics and Leadership:**
  Delve into the nuances of effective team management and leadership, nurturing a collaborative and productive work environment.

- **Forming:**
  In the forming stage, team members come together, get acquainted, and establish initial impressions. They may be polite and cautious in their interactions as they begin to understand their roles and expectations within the team. Leadership during this stage involves providing guidance and clarity on the team's purpose and objectives.

- **Storming:**
  The storming stage is characterized by increased conflict and competition among team members. As individuals express their opinions and ideas, differences may arise. Effective leaders during this stage encourage open communication, address conflicts constructively, and guide the team toward resolutions that foster collaboration.

- **Norming:**
  In the norming stage, the team starts to resolve conflicts, establish norms, and develop a sense of cohesion. Members begin to appreciate each other's strengths and work more collaboratively. Leadership at this stage involves reinforcing positive behaviors, facilitating communication, and nurturing a supportive team culture.

- **Performing:**
  The performing stage represents the peak of the team's effectiveness. Team members work seamlessly together, leveraging their strengths to achieve common goals. Leadership in this stage involves empowering team members, providing autonomy, and ensuring that resources are available to maintain high performance.

- **Adjourning:**
  The adjourning stage occurs when the team completes its project or mission. Also known as the "mourning" stage, this involves acknowledging achievements,

recognizing contributions, and preparing for team members to transition to new roles or projects. Leadership during this stage may include facilitating closure, celebrating successes, and addressing any emotional aspects of the team's disbandment.

INFUSING DETERMINATION INTO RELATIONSHIP BUILDING

- **The Role of Determination:**
  Grasp how your determination and perseverance stand as pivotal assets in relationship building. We'll dissect the significance of unwavering commitment, especially when confronted with challenges or setbacks.

- **Effective Communication:**
  Master the art of articulating your vision and values to your team, partners, and vendors. Effective communication lays the bedrock for forging enduring and robust relationships.

- **Networking and Community Engagement:**
  Unearth the transformative potential of networking and community engagement in expanding your entrepreneurial support network. Gain insights into engaging with local business communities and industry-specific networks.

BUILDING YOUR ENTREPRENEURIAL SUPPORT NETWORK

Whether you are a team, partner, or vendor, don't hesitate to speak up when constructing your support network. There's no need to fear asking the wrong question at the wrong time or from the wrong person. If a door closes, move on to the next one. Embrace rejection as a stepping stone to improvement.

PHASES OF BUILDING AN ENTREPRENEURIAL GOAL OR COMPANY:

Embarking on the journey of building an entrepreneurial venture is a dynamic process marked by distinct phases, each crucial to the overall success of the endeavor. These five phases serve as a roadmap for aspiring entrepreneurs, guiding them from an idea's inception to a company's flourishing growth. Let's delve into the key stages:

- **Idea Generation and Brainstorming:**
  The entrepreneurial journey often begins with a spark of creativity. Aspiring entrepreneurs engage in idea generation and brainstorming sessions in this initial phase. They explore innovative concepts, identify market needs, and conceptualize solutions that form the foundation of their entrepreneurial goals.

- **Opportunity Evaluation:**
  With ideas in hand, entrepreneurs move into the phase of opportunity evaluation. This involves a comprehensive analysis of the market landscape, potential competitors, and the feasibility of turning ideas into viable business opportunities. Entrepreneurs assess the viability and potential success of their concepts in the current business environment.

- **Planning and Development:**
  Successful entrepreneurship hinges on meticulous planning and development. In this phase, entrepreneurs translate their ideas into actionable plans. They outline business strategies, establish goals, and develop a roadmap for execution. Attention to detail is crucial as entrepreneurs lay the groundwork for the practical implementation of their vision.

- **Company Formation:**
  As plans solidify, the entrepreneurial journey advances

to the formalization of the business entity. Company formation involves legal and organizational processes, such as registering the business, defining the corporate structure, and establishing the necessary frameworks for operations. Entrepreneurs navigate the administrative steps required to bring their vision to life.

- **Launch and Growth:**
  The culmination of efforts leads to the exciting phase of launch and growth. Entrepreneurs introduce their products or services to the market, leveraging their planning and development phases. The focus shifts to customer acquisition, market penetration, and sustained growth. This phase requires adaptability and strategic decision-making to navigate the challenges and opportunities that arise.

FOSTERING RELATIONSHIPS WITH PARTNERS AND VENDORS

- **Strategic Alliances:**
  Explore the perks of forging strategic alliances with other businesses and entrepreneurs. Uncover how these relationships can extend your reach, pool resources, and unlock new vistas of opportunity.

- **Vendor Relationships:**
  Learn how to establish and sustain robust connections with vendors, suppliers, and service providers. These relationships form the lifeblood of your business's operational smoothness.

- **Negotiation Skills:**
  Acquire insights into negotiation strategies that pave the way for mutually beneficial partnerships, securing favorable terms with vendors and collaborators.

- **Accommodating:**
  Accommodating is a negotiation style characterized by a

high level of cooperativeness and a low level of assertiveness. In this approach, individuals prioritize maintaining relationships and satisfying the other party's needs, often at the expense of their own objectives. It is effective when preserving relationships is crucial.

- **Avoiding:**
  Avoiding is a strategy where individuals choose not to engage in the negotiation process. This style is characterized by low assertiveness and low cooperativeness. It might be employed when the issue is not significant or when temporarily avoiding conflict is deemed more beneficial than immediate resolution.

- **Collaborating:**
  Collaborating is a high assertiveness and high cooperativeness negotiation style. It involves a mutual effort to find a solution that fully satisfies the concerns and interests of all parties. Collaboration often leads to creative and long-lasting solutions, making it an effective approach in complex or integrative negotiations.

- **Competing:**
  Competing is a highly assertive and low-cooperative negotiation style. It involves pursuing one's goals at the expense of the other party's interests. This approach is useful when immediate action is required or when one party has a stronger position of power.

- **Compromising:**
  Compromising strikes a balance between assertiveness and cooperativeness. Both parties make concessions to achieve a middle ground in this negotiation style. While it may not result in an ideal solution for either side, compromising ensures a quick resolution and is suitable for situations where time is a critical factor.

Chapter Summary

Chapter 7 is your handbook for cultivating and nurturing your entrepreneurial support network. From crafting a capable team to forming strategic alliances with partners and vendors, this chapter offers invaluable counsel on establishing a network that propels your business forward. Your determination and effective communication skills are potent tools in this process. As you wrap up this chapter, you'll possess a clear roadmap for leveraging your determination and networking understanding, setting the stage for collaborative success in your entrepreneurial odyssey.

8 ELEVATING YOUR SALES AND MARKETING MASTERY

"Scaling your business is the ascension into a transformative phase. It's about making decisions, mastering resources, and navigating global ventures with determination, turning challenges into opportunities."

In Chapter 8, we immerse ourselves in the indispensable realms of mastering sales and marketing as an entrepreneur. These twin pillars are the lifeblood of your business, and this chapter serves as your compass in attracting your audience. We'll unravel the nuances of understanding your target audience, offer real-world examples and case studies, and underscore the enduring value of perseverance in your sales and marketing endeavors.

THE SYMPHONY OF SALES AND MARKETING:

CAPTIVATING YOUR AUDIENCE

- **Understanding Your Target Audience:**
  Commence your journey by delving into the pivotal process of understanding your audience. We'll explore the critical art of identifying your ideal customers, discerning their needs, and aligning your product or service to offer seamless solutions.

- **Demographic:**
  Demographic segmentation involves categorizing the target market based on quantifiable characteristics such as age, gender, income, education level, occupation, and family status. This information helps businesses tailor their marketing efforts to specific demographic groups with similar needs and preferences.

- **Geographic:**
  Geographic segmentation involves dividing the target market based on geographic locations, such as country, region, city, or climate. Understanding the geographical aspects of the market is crucial for adapting marketing strategies to regional preferences and local trends.

- **Psychographic:**
  Psychographic segmentation delves into the psychological and lifestyle aspects of the target market. This includes values, interests, attitudes, hobbies, and personality traits. By understanding the psychographics of their audience, businesses can create more personalized and resonant marketing messages.

- **Behavioral:**
  Behavioral segmentation focuses on consumer behavior and patterns. This includes analyzing purchasing habits, product usage, brand loyalty, and other behaviors related to the buying decision. Businesses use this information to tailor marketing strategies that align with the preferences and behaviors of their target audience.

- **Crafting a Captivating Value Proposition:**
  Learn how to fashion a unique and compelling value proposition, a beacon that sets your business apart and resonates profoundly with your target audience.

- **Diverse Marketing Channels and Strategies:**
  Navigate through a spectrum of marketing channels and strategies, from the digital realm and content marketing to the traditional advertising avenues. Discover how to handpick the most potent channels for reaching your audience effectively.

- **Product:**
  The product element focuses on developing and presenting a desirable and valuable offering to the target market. This includes the product's features, design, quality, and how it fulfills customer needs. Successful

marketing hinges on understanding and effectively communicating the unique selling propositions of a product.

- **Price:**
Price is a critical aspect of marketing strategy, influencing consumer perception and purchasing decisions. The pricing strategy should align with the product's value proposition, target market expectations, and overall business objectives. Strategies may include competitive pricing, penetration pricing, or premium pricing.

- **Promotion:**
Promotion involves communicating and promoting the product to the target audience. This includes advertising, public relations, sales promotions, and other communication efforts. The goal is to create awareness, generate interest, and drive customer action. Promotion strategies should be tailored to the target market's characteristics and the product.

- **Place:**
Place, also known as distribution, focuses on making the product accessible to customers. This involves selecting the right distribution channels through direct sales, retailers, e-commerce platforms, or other intermediaries. The goal is to ensure the product is available for the customer at the right place and time.

- **People:**
The people element recognizes the impact of customer service, relationships, and employee engagement on the success of a marketing strategy. Building positive customer relationships, providing excellent customer service, and ensuring employees are knowledgeable and aligned with brand values contribute to overall marketing success.

PERSEVERANCE IN THE SALES AND MARKETING ODYSSEY:
STAYING TRUE TO THE COURSE

- **A Long-Term Perspective:**
  Absorb the wisdom that successful sales and marketing transcend quick wins—it's about cultivating enduring relationships with customers. We'll explore the significance of adopting long-term strategies and unwavering commitment to your marketing endeavors.

- **Adaptability Amidst Market Fluctuations:**
  The entrepreneurial landscape often demands navigating shifts in market dynamics. Learn how to adapt your sales and marketing strategies to stay relevant and competitive amidst evolving environments.

- **Resilience in the Face of Rejection:**
  Sale is an arena with its share of challenges. Unearth strategies for nurturing resilience when confronted with rejection, and discover how setbacks can be springboards for growth.

- **Mastery in Sales and Marketing:**
  Two archetypes emerge in the realm of sales: personal or consumer sales and corporate or company sales. I lean towards personal sales, where decisions are swift and layers of decision-making are minimal. Our primary focus for insurance products and services centers on consumer and small business sales, often characterized by quicker decisions.

EXEMPLARY CASE STUDIES IN EFFECTIVE MARKETING

- **Real-World Triumphs:**
  Immerse yourself in the wisdom gleaned from real-world examples and case studies of entrepreneurs who have

wielded marketing strategies with finesse to propel their businesses forward. These narratives offer both inspiration and actionable takeaways.

- **Measuring the Marketing Tapestry:**
  Grasp the importance of tracking and measuring your marketing efforts. We'll explore key performance indicators (KPIs) and tools for meticulously evaluating your marketing campaign's return on investment (ROI).

- **Leveraging Technology's Embrace:**
  Explore how the tapestry of technology can be woven into your entrepreneurial fabric, automating marketing processes, refining customer relationship management, and amplifying the overall efficacy of your marketing initiatives.

Chapter Summary

Chapter 8 casts a spotlight on the art of mastering sales and marketing, pivotal elements in the tapestry of entrepreneurship. This chapter is your guide to attracting and retaining customers, from decoding your target audience to crafting compelling value propositions and deploying effective marketing strategies. Real-world examples and case studies offer pragmatic insights, while the enduring theme of perseverance underscores its necessity for long-term success. As you navigate through this chapter, you'll gain profound insights into leveraging sales and marketing as formidable instruments in your entrepreneurial repertoire.

9 NAVIGATING THE HEIGHTS - SCALING AND EXPANDING YOUR BUSINESS

"Entrepreneurial legacy is not just about financial success; it's about leaving an indelible mark on your industry, community, and the next generation. Succession planning and mentorship are the threads that weave this legacy."

In Chapter 9, we plunge into the exhilarating yet intricate process of scaling and expanding your business. Scaling marks a pivotal milestone in your entrepreneurial odyssey, and this chapter unfolds insights into steering the growth of your venture. We explore the diverse avenues of expansion, the challenges and opportunities accompanying global outreach, and the unwavering role of determination in this transformative phase.

ASCENSION BEGINS:

CULTIVATING GROWTH IN YOUR ENTREPRENEURIAL VENTURE

- **The Decision-Making Crucible:**
  We embark on this journey by dissecting the pivotal decision-making process behind scaling your business. What are the telltale signs that your business is poised for expansion? We delve into various scaling models, including horizontal and vertical expansion, franchising, and more.

- **Resource Mastery:**
  Learn the art of effectively allocating resources—finances, personnel, and infrastructure—to fortify the growth of your business. Discover strategies for

optimizing efficiency during this metamorphic phase.

- **Guardianship of Quality:**
  Understand the significance of preserving the quality of your products or services as you traverse the expansion trajectory. We dissect how consistency and upholding your brand's integrity become linchpins in sustaining growth.

CHALLENGES AND OPPORTUNITIES OF GLOBAL EXPEDITION

- **Global Ventures:**
  For those with aspirations stretching beyond local confines, we unravel the challenges and opportunities entwined with global expansion. Learn how to adapt to different cultural, legal, and economic landscapes.

- **Market Mastery and Adaptation:**
  Plunge into the critical role of market research when venturing into new territories. Comprehend the art of adapting your business model and marketing strategies to harmonize with international audiences.

- **Risk Sailing:**
  As you sail on the seas of expansion, risk management becomes the guiding North Star. We navigate through strategies to assess and mitigate the risks associated with expansion, from currency fluctuations to political turbulences.

HARVESTING WITH DETERMINATION: SCALING AS AN ODYSSEY

- **The Determination Crucible:**
  Scaling your business demands fortitude. In this segment, we delve into the significance of determination and resilience. Hear stories of entrepreneurs who faced obstacles but persisted, ultimately achieving remarkable

success.

- **Mentorship Odyssey:**
  Uncover how mentorship and perpetual learning can fuel your scaling success. We explore the wisdom of seeking advice and insights from seasoned entrepreneurs as an invaluable compass.

- **Equilibrium Dance:**
  Strike the delicate balance between growth and sustainability. Understand how to ensure your business grows and sustains its expansion, continuing to flourish.

- **Diversification and Adaptation: Navigating Uncharted Waters:**
  Some businesses falter because, in their prime, they failed to diversify or adapt to a changing environment. Environments evolve due to trends, habits, technology, or becoming obsolete. In this section, we unravel stories of businesses that thrived or faltered based on their adaptability and diversification strategies.

Chapter Summary

Chapter 9 unfolds as a comprehensive guide through the critical juncture of scaling and expanding your entrepreneurial voyage. This chapter offers invaluable insights from the inception of the decision to grow, resource management, and global forays. Determination and resilience stand as guiding beacons as you navigate the intricate dance between challenges and opportunities. By the chapter's end, you'll be well-prepared to elevate your business to new heights, ensuring its sustained success.

10 CRAFTING YOUR ENTREPRENEURIAL LEGACY

"As an entrepreneur, your legacy goes beyond the business; it's a tapestry woven with purpose, mentorship, and meticulous planning. Craft it with determination, leaving an impact that transcends generations."

Chapter 10 takes a profound dive into the concept of the entrepreneurial legacy, aiming to unravel personal success and the enduring impact you can leave on your business, community, and future generations of entrepreneurs. This chapter navigates through the multifaceted facets of entrepreneurial legacy, succession planning, and the profound significance of passing the torch to future leaders.

THE ENTREPRENEURIAL LEGACY:
A TAPESTRY BEYOND FINANCES

- **Defining Entrepreneurial Legacy:**
  The journey begins by delving deep into the essence of an entrepreneurial legacy, transcending financial success. It encompasses the influence etched on your industry, community, and the lives you've touched. The narrative emphasizes the importance of purpose-driven entrepreneurship, leaving a mark beyond monetary achievements.

- **Small Business Entrepreneurship:**
  Small business entrepreneurship involves creating and operating small-scale enterprises, often within local communities. These entrepreneurs focus on meeting the needs of a specific market, providing essential goods or services, and contributing to the economic vitality of their community. The legacy of small business

entrepreneurship often lies in fostering local connections and sustaining community well-being.

- **Scalable Startup Entrepreneurship:**
  Scalable startup entrepreneurship is characterized by the pursuit of rapid growth and scalability. Entrepreneurs in this category aim to create innovative products or services with the potential to reach a large market. The legacy of scalable startups often revolves around technological advancements, market disruption, and the creation of new industries.

- **Social Entrepreneurship:**
  Social entrepreneurship addresses social or environmental challenges through innovative business models. Entrepreneurs in this realm aim to create a positive and sustainable impact alongside financial success. The positive changes in society or the environment often measure the legacy of social entrepreneurship.

- **Large Company Entrepreneurship:**
  Large company entrepreneurship, also known as corporate entrepreneurship or "intrapreneurship," involves fostering an entrepreneurial spirit within established organizations. This form of entrepreneurship encourages employees to innovate, take risks, and develop new products or services within the corporate structure. The legacy of large company entrepreneurship lies in fostering a culture of innovation, adaptability, and continued growth within established enterprises.

CHARACTERISTICS INCREASING ENTREPRENEURS' CHANCE OF ACCOMPLISHING LONG-TERM SUCCESS:

Embarking on the entrepreneurial journey demands a unique set of characteristics that significantly influence an individual's ability to achieve long-term success. As entrepreneurs navigate the challenges and opportunities inherent in the business landscape, certain traits become crucial in shaping the trajectory of their ventures. Let's explore these key characteristics that enhance the likelihood of accomplishing enduring success:

- **Time is Essence:**
  In the realm of entrepreneurship, time is a precious commodity. Successful entrepreneurs understand the value of time management. The ability to prioritize tasks, set realistic deadlines, and optimize efficiency contributes to the overall effectiveness of their endeavors. Entrepreneurial success often hinges on making strategic decisions promptly, capitalizing on market trends, and adapting swiftly to changes.

- **Stress Management:**
  The entrepreneurial journey is marked by uncertainties, challenges, and high-pressure situations. Entrepreneurs who excel in stress management are better equipped to navigate these complexities. Cultivating resilience, maintaining composure under pressure, and developing coping mechanisms are essential for long-term success. Effective stress management enables entrepreneurs to make informed decisions and lead their ventures with clarity.

- **Sales, Marketing, and Networking Abilities:**
  The ability to sell products or services, market effectively, and build strong networks is fundamental to

entrepreneurial success. Entrepreneurs must possess sales acumen to convey the value of their offerings, implement strategic marketing initiatives, and cultivate meaningful connections within their industry. These skills amplify brand visibility, foster customer relationships, and open doors to collaboration and growth.

- **Money and Reserve Fund:**
  Financial acuity is a cornerstone of entrepreneurial success. Effective financial management involves not only generating revenue but also prudently allocating resources and building a reserve fund. Entrepreneurs with a keen understanding of their financial landscape are better positioned to weather economic fluctuations, invest strategically, and sustain their ventures through both lean and prosperous times.

- **Faith and Belief:**
  Entrepreneurial journeys are fraught with uncertainties, requiring a steadfast belief in one's vision and capabilities. Entrepreneurs who maintain unwavering faith in their goals, even in the face of setbacks, are more resilient. This belief serves as a driving force, propelling them to overcome challenges, persevere through adversity, and stay committed to the long-term success of their ventures.

INSPIRING OTHERS: A RIPPLE EFFECT OF INFLUENCE

- **Your Journey as a Beacon:**
  Your entrepreneurial odyssey serves as a powerful source of inspiration for others. The chapter unfolds the pivotal role of mentorship, the art of story-sharing, and the responsibility of giving back to the entrepreneurial community.

SUCCESSION PLANNING AND ESTATE CRAFTING

- **Passing the Torch:**
  Succession planning is a cornerstone in preserving your business legacy. The chapter navigates the crucial steps in priming your business for a seamless transition to the next generation of leaders or new ownership.

- **Estate Planning:**
  Beyond business, estate planning ensures that your assets align with your wishes. Essential topics like wills, trusts, and the strategic importance of early planning are unveiled to secure a holistic legacy.

- **Family Business Dynamics:**
  For those steering family businesses, unique considerations are addressed. The chapter delves into navigating the complexities of transferring ownership within a family, maintaining harmony, and ensuring sustained success.

A LEGACY FORGED IN DETERMINATION

- **The Mentorship Landscape:**
  The narrative unfolds the profound significance of mentoring and offering guidance to aspiring entrepreneurs. Discover how your knowledge and experiences can mold the next generation of business leaders.

- **Interest:**
  Interest is the foundational pillar of mentorship, emphasizing the mentor's genuine concern for the mentee's development and success. A mentor who takes a sincere interest in the mentee's goals, challenges, and aspirations lays the groundwork for a meaningful and impactful mentorship relationship.

- **Investment:**
  Investment in mentorship goes beyond mere time and resources; it involves a commitment to the mentee's growth and development. A mentor who invests in the mentee's success provides guidance, shares knowledge, and offers support, actively contributing to the mentee's professional and personal advancement.

- **Involvement:**
  Involvement in mentorship signifies active engagement and participation. Mentors who are involved regularly communicate with their mentees, offer constructive feedback, and actively contribute to the mentee's learning journey. This active involvement fosters a sense of accountability and connection.

- **Inculcation:**
  Inculcation refers to the process of instilling values, skills, and knowledge in the mentee. Mentors are crucial in guiding mentees to develop critical skills, ethical values, and a strong work ethic. Inculcation is about imparting wisdom and experiences that contribute to the mentee's growth.

- **Inspiration:**
  Inspiration is a powerful pillar that motivates and empowers mentees to reach their full potential. Mentors who inspire their mentees contribute to their self-confidence, ambition, and resilience. By setting an example and sharing their experiences, mentors can ignite a sense of purpose and determination in their mentees.

- **Values Transference:**
  Passing the torch extends to instilling the values and work ethic pivotal to your success. The chapter unravels strategies to ensure that these principles endure, maintaining the integrity of your legacy.

- **Continuity of Impact:**
Leaving a legacy is not the conclusion but a new beginning. The chapter discusses how you can continue to play a pivotal role in your business or community even after transitioning to the next phase of life.

A LEGACY IN PROGRESS:

THE STORY OF AMAZING INSURANCE SERVICES, LLC

- **Perpetuating the Brand:**
Entrepreneurs like Amazing Insurance Services, LLC., face crucial decisions regarding their legacy. The chapter reflects on the aspiration to perpetuate the company name, brand, and agency. Exploring options from qualified management to potential partnerships highlights the intricate balance between scale, community impact, and retaining the brand's essence.

- **The Heart of the Matter:**
The chapter underlines that Amazing Insurance Services, LLC. is not just a commodity for sale; it's a social entrepreneurial endeavor. The brand holds the biggest asset—community trust, integrity, morals, and a history of active community participation. The journey entails exploring avenues like venture capitalists, angel investors, or incubators, always aiming to retain control of the name and brand.

- **Culmination:**
Chapter 10 serves as a guide to shape your entrepreneurial legacy, weaving it into a tapestry that transcends financial success. It underscores the importance of purpose, mentorship, and meticulous planning in creating a lasting impact. As you navigate the complexities of succession planning and reflect on the values that define your legacy, this chapter empowers

you to leave a mark that extends far beyond the realms of entrepreneurship.

MY TAKEAWAYS:

INSIGHTS FROM A SUCCESSFUL AND EXPERIENCED ENTREPRENEUR

Entrepreneurship involves the intricate process of creating and establishing a new business venture with the primary objectives of generating profit, fostering job creation in the community, and delivering value to customers. This entrepreneurial journey is marked by a unique blend of challenges and opportunities, making it a transformative experience.

While the path to success in entrepreneurship is seldom straightforward, it offers numerous valuable lessons along the way. Adequate preparation, thorough research, and meticulous planning before embarking on this journey can safeguard against potential setbacks and failures.

For entrepreneurs, a willingness to take risks is paramount, whether those risks are deemed small, moderate, or high. Embracing and learning from mistakes, coupled with the ability to adapt to dynamic market conditions, are crucial elements of entrepreneurial resilience. Here are some key takeaways gleaned from the experiences of a successful entrepreneur.

- **A Winning Mindset – A Burning Desire for Success:**
  Entrepreneurs must embody a winning mindset, possessing confidence, emotional resilience, and the ability to initiate and navigate a venture from its inception to fruition despite challenges. Depending on the organization's nature, depth, or size, each entrepreneurial journey presents its unique set of challenges, setbacks, and opportunities. It resembles a puzzle waiting to be meticulously pieced together, one

step at a time, like ascending a staircase.

- **Guided by Vision, Purpose, & Passion:**
  Entrepreneurs should have a well-defined purpose and
  be passionate about their vision or business endeavors.
  Confronted with obstacles, entrepreneurs driven by
  passion and purpose are more likely to persevere until
  they achieve their goals. Without a clear objective, the
  risk of giving up or losing direction becomes more
  pronounced.

- **Visualize Your Future & Accelerate Your
  Journey:**
  Even before embarking on the entrepreneurial journey,
  entrepreneurs must visualize their daily activities,
  including the type of work, hours, responsibilities,
  difficulties, and rewards. Failing to do so may lead to
  realizations that come too late. Entrepreneurs must be
  able to foresee and feel their journey, ensuring they
  clearly understand what lies ahead. For instance,
  choosing a rundown location without careful
  consideration can permanently jeopardize the business's
  survivability, even if the rent is affordable, due to a lack
  of traffic or demographic support.

- **Focus on Your End Result & Ultimate
  Destination:**
  Define your ultimate goal, destination, or result. Do you
  aspire to be a regular, average boxer, an amateur, or a
  heavyweight champion? Proper preparation significantly
  increases the chances of success, making entrepreneurs
  need to know their desired result, backtrack, and build
  their future.

- **Timeline & Deadline:**
  A sense of urgency is imperative, as entrepreneurs don't
  have the luxury of waiting indefinitely. It's a now-or-
  never situation, as opportunities, leases, and business
  ventures may slip away if not seized promptly.

Opportunities knock once, and entrepreneurs must capture the right moment.

- **Setbacks & Failure:**
  Failure is an inherent part of the entrepreneurial journey. It's crucial to perceive failure as an opportunity to learn and grow stronger. Successful entrepreneurs view failure as a means to refine their approaches and strategies and fortify their operations.

Do You Possess the Qualities to Overcome Your Challenges?

It can be self-discipline, determination, knowledge, financial resources, manpower, location, or connections to inventory sources. While everyone desires success, not everyone possesses the necessary qualifications.

With an abundance of Patience, Perseverance, and endurance:

Entrepreneurs must exhibit exceptional patience to endure and move forward in industries like insurance and financial services, where the job can be monotonous. Many individuals change jobs within three years, and few last beyond five years. Anything exceeding that marks a career or a lifelong venture.

Powerful Teamwork & Empowerment:

Recruiting and finding qualified individuals is no easy task; thus, teamwork is crucial in entrepreneurship or business. Surrounding yourself with a team of talented individuals who share your vision and complement your strengths is key to achieving success and sustaining a long-term endeavor.

Quality Customer Service & Support:

Successful entrepreneurs prioritize their customers, listening to their needs, understanding pain points, and developing solutions that address those needs. When customer needs are met, they retain their clientele and receive referrals.

Focusing on customer needs is pivotal in building a profitable business.

Adaptability to Change & Adjustment to New Environments:

The business landscape is ever-evolving, demanding adaptability from entrepreneurs. Change is inevitable; regardless of its nature, every business requires change to survive. Successful entrepreneurs pivot their business models, adjust strategies, and embrace new technologies and trends. They continually learn, grow, and evolve to stay ahead of the competition.

Business & Community Networking:

Strong networking is crucial for success in entrepreneurship or business—it's not a choice but a necessity. Building a robust network of mentors, advisors, and peers can offer valuable guidance, support, and resources. Successful individuals leverage their networks to gain insights, make connections, and grow their enterprises.

Commitment & Dedication:

Entrepreneurship is a lifelong journey, demanding hard work, dedication, and perseverance. Successful entrepreneurs remain committed to their vision, mission, and objectives. They maintain a positive mindset, stay motivated, and keep charging forward.

Entrepreneurship is a rewarding yet challenging journey requiring passion, purpose, hard work, focus, and perseverance. Entrepreneurs can build successful businesses by prioritizing customer needs, forming a strong team, adapting to change, and viewing failure as an opportunity to learn and improve. With commitment, dedication, hard work, and a willingness to learn, anyone can become a successful entrepreneur over time.

VARIOUS BUSINESS MODELS

People who want maximum freedom create their businesses or brands if they wish for creativity and total management control.

People who want maximum freedom create their own businesses or brands. Suppose they want creativity and total management control. People who don't mind following directions or instructions can use the captive or franchise model. They don't need to figure anything out; just follow the process. The good thing is they have a systematic way to do things and grow the business. Franchise has certain requirements: experience, expertise, minimum financial investment, franchise fee, and financial/asset qualification. Different businesses and franchisors have different requirements. For example, Subway, before you open the door, you have to spend X amount of money to remodel, buy equipment, and have enough reserve funds to operate.

ENTREPRENEURS & SMALL BUSINESSES STATISTICS OVERVIEW:

Being an Entrepreneur:

- 96% of self-employed individuals prefer staying self-employed over returning to a full-time job.

- 1 in 5 entrepreneurs owns or manages a business with family members.

- 58% of entrepreneurs have previous experience working in the corporate world before venturing into entrepreneurship.

Success Rates of Entrepreneurs:

- According to NBCS, only 40% of small businesses generate a profit.

- Approximately 30% of businesses break even, while the remaining 30% incur losses.

Failure Rates of Entrepreneurs:

- The failure rate is 20% in the first year.

- Half of the businesses are still operational after five years.

Common Reasons for Small Business Failure (according to business owners):

- Running out of money

- Being in the wrong market

- Lack of research

- Bad partnerships

- Ineffective marketing

- Not being an expert in the field

Key Quality of an Entrepreneur:

- Self-discipline is the ability to work persistently, even when motivation is lacking. Entrepreneurs often work longer hours, necessitating self-motivation to succeed.

Ownership Distribution in Small Businesses:

- Women own 42% of all small businesses, totaling 13 million woman-owned businesses.

- These businesses collectively employ over 94 million workers.

Education:

- 44% of entrepreneurs have a college degree.

RESOURCE GUIDE:

- U.S. Small Business Administration
  409 3rd St., SW Washington, DC 20416
  800-827-5722
  www.sba.gov

- California Office of the Small Business Advocate (CalOSBA)
  1325 J Street, Suite 1800 Sacramento, CA 95814
  1-877-345-4633
  www.calosba.ca.gov

- SCORE/ The SCORE Foundation
  1165 Herndon Parkway, Suite 100 Herndon, VA 20170
  1-800-634-0245
  www.score.org / www.scorefoundation.org

- U.S. Department of Commerce
  1401 Constitution Ave, NW Washington, DC 20230
  www.commerce.gov

- U.S. Department of State
  Entrepreneurship – United States Department of State
  OSDBU, SA-6, Room L500 Washington, DC 20522
  703-875-6822
  www.state.gov

- U.S. Department of the Treasury
  1500 Pennsylvania Ave, NW Washington, DC 20220
  202-622-2000
  home.treasury.gov

- Insurance Information Institute
  110 William Street New York, NY 10038

212-346-5500

www.iii.org

- Secretary of State

  1500 11th St Sacramento, CA 95814

  916-657-5448

  www.sos.ca.gov

- Internal Revenue Service, IRS

  4330-Watt Ave Sacramento, CA 95821

  844-545-5640

  www.irs.gov

- Franchise Tax Board

  3321 Power Inn Road, Suite 250 Sacramento, CA 95826

  916-227-6822

  www.ftb.ca.gov

- Sacramento Entrepreneurship Academy (SEA)

  502 Mace Blvd Davis, CA 95616

  916-291-2740

  www.sealink.org

- UC Davis Institute for Innovation and Entrepreneurship

  University of California, Davis

  540 Alumni Lane Davis, CA 95616

  530-564-2327

  https://innovate.ucdavis.edu/academy

- Young Entrepreneur Academy, Inc.

  1008 W Avenue M-4 Ste A Palmdale, CA 93551

  661-948-4518/585-981-1818

  info@yeausa.org

https://yeausa.org/

- California State Controller

  300 Capitol Mall, Suite 1850 Sacramento, CA 95814

  916-445-2636

  www.sco.ca.gov

- Bunker Labs, a national non-profit.

  230 E Ohio St, Suite 410 # 1241 Chicago, Illinois 60611

  www.bunkerlabs.org

- BNI

  11525 North Community House Road, Suite 475 Charlotte, NC 28277

  800-825-8286

  www.bni.com

- Venture Lab for children

  www.venturelab.org

- National Nurse Practitioner Entrepreneur Network

  860-322-0708

  https://nnpen.org/contact

- Community Development Venture Capital Alliance

  475 Riverside Drive, Suite 1264, New York, NY 10115

  cdvca@cdvca.org

  www.cdvca.org

- National Restaurant Association

  2055 L Street NW, Suite 700, Washington, DC 20036

  202-331-5900/800-424-5156

  www.restaurant.org

- Entrepreneurs Organization

  500 Montgomery Street, Suite 600, Alexandria, VA 22314

  703-519-6700

  https://hub.eonetwork.org

- Farm Foundation

  1301 West 22nd St, Suite 906, Oak Brook, IL
  60523-2197

  www.farmfoundation.org

- U.S. Chamber of Commerce

  1615 H Street, NW Washington, DC 20062-2000

  202-689-6000

  800-638-6582

  www.uschamber.com

- National Federation of Independent Business Tennessee

  800-634-2669

  www.nfib.com

- National Retail Federation

  202 York Ave NW Suite 1200 Washington, DC 20005

  202-783-7971/800-673-4692

  www.nrf.com

- American Marketing Association

  800-AMA-1150

  www.ama.org

- International Franchise Association

  1900 K St, NW Suite 700 Washington, DC 20006

  202-628-8000

  www.franchise.org

- Office of the Comptroller of the Currency
  400 7th St. SW Washington, DC 20219
  202-649-6800
  www.occ.gov
- United States Telecom Association
  1400 16th St NW # 600 Washington, DC 20036
  202-736-3200
  www.ctia.org
- Toastmasters International
  9127 S Jamacia Street, Suite 400 Englewood, CO 80112
  720-439-5050
  www.toastmasters.org
- Better Business Bureau – BBB
  703-276-0100
  www.bbb.org
- Ewing Marion Kauffman Foundation Non-profit
  4801 Rockhill Road Kansas City, MO 64110
  www.kauffman.org
- California Green Business Network General Info
  info@greenbusinessca.org
  www.greenbusinessca.org
- Give Back Nation
  National HQ in Orlando, FL
  grow@givebacknation.com
  888-894-7261
  www.givebacknation.com

- Working for Women

  PO Box 1309 Kingston, NY 12402

  845-206-9920

  www.workingforwomen.org

- Seed SPOT

  515 E Grant Street, Suite 150 Phoenix, AZ 85004

  602-456-9944 (Call or Tex)

  connect@seedspot.org

  www.seedspot.org

- U.S. Department of Health and Human Services

  200 Independence Avenue, S.W. Washington, DC 20201

  877-696-6775

  www.hhs.gov

- U.S. General Services Administration

  844-GSA-4111

  www.gsa.gov

- The Federal Deposit Insurance Corporation (FDIC)

  FDIC – Small Business

  550 17th Street, NW, F-6000 Washington, DC 20429

  877-275-3342

  www.fdic.gov

- Secretary of Homeland Security

  Small Business Assistance Washington, DC 20528

  202-282-8000

  www.dhs.gov/small-business-assistance

- FEMA Small Business Program

  500 C Street, SW Washington, DC 20472-3210

  202-646-2500

  Hotline: 800-621-3362

  https://www.fema.gov/business-industry/doing-business/small-business

- Department of Labor

  200 Constitution Ave NW Washington, DC 20210

  866-487-2365

  www.dol.gov

- California Capital Financial Development Corporation

  1792 Tribute Road, Suite 270

  Sacramento, CA 95815

  916-442-1729

  www.cacapital.org

- Grow America

  633 Third Ave, 19th Fl, Suite J New York, NY 10017

  800-501-7489

  www.growamerica.org

- America's SBDC

  www.americassbdc.org

CONCLUSION

As we reach the culmination of this entrepreneurial journey, it is not merely the end of a book but the commencement of an empowered venture. The chapters have unfolded a narrative rich with insights, experiences, and guidance, providing you with a compass to navigate the unpredictable seas of entrepreneurship. Let's reflect on the key takeaways and the spirit that propels your odyssey.

The Entrepreneurial Mindset:

Embracing the entrepreneurial mindset is not just about starting a business; it's a way of approaching challenges as opportunities, cultivating resilience, and consistently seeking growth. Your attitude shapes the trajectory of your journey, turning setbacks into stepping stones and obstacles into innovation.

1. **Guiding the Entrepreneurial Odyssey: Nurturing Growth and Resilience:**

   Chapter 1: In this transformative chapter, we delve into the essence of entrepreneurship, unveiling the significance of self-evaluation and personal development as the guiding compass through the dynamic landscape of business. The narrative accentuates the pivotal role of self-awareness, work ethics, commitment, expertise, and connections in unlocking the latent entrepreneurial potential. We explore the strategic impact of location on business trajectories and provide insights into the art of choosing the optimal environment. This chapter is a comprehensive guide from navigating the entrepreneurial grind to mastering the delicate equilibrium between ambition and patience. As we embark on this transformative journey, let's collectively unlock our potential, cultivate resilience, and set the stage for unparalleled personal and professional metamorphosis.

2. **Empowering Entrepreneurship: A Navigational Blueprint for Minorities:**
   Chapter 2: As we traverse the extensive resource guide tailored for minority entrepreneurs, the overarching theme is one of empowerment, fostering connections, and accessing vital organizational support. From the venerable Minority Business Development Agency to local chambers of commerce, this guide unfolds a roadmap for minorities to harness robust support systems. Each entry represents a potential stepping stone toward success, whether through mentorship, financial opportunities, or active community engagement. By tapping into these invaluable resources, entrepreneurs can adeptly navigate challenges, seize opportunities, and contribute to a more inclusive and dynamic business landscape. This comprehensive guide is an earnest invitation to leverage the collective strength of support and embark on a transformative journey of entrepreneurship that transcends conventional boundaries.

3. **Navigating Risks and Embracing Preparedness:**
   Chapter 3 equipped you with the tools to navigate risks and embrace preparedness. Your ability to assess personal and financial readiness, understand market dynamics, and create a support system lays the foundation for a robust entrepreneurial venture. Remember, entrepreneurship is an adventure; embrace the challenges, and let perseverance be your guiding light.

4. **Problem-Solving in Entrepreneurship:**
   Chapter 4 delved into the intricate world of facing financial challenges, adapting to market changes, overcoming operational obstacles, and mastering the art of customer satisfaction. Each challenge is an opportunity for growth, and your proactive approach

can transform obstacles into stepping stones toward lasting success.

5. **Tales of Triumph and Unyielding Resilience:**
Chapter 5 explored genuine narratives from entrepreneurs who triumphed over adversities. Their stories are beacons of inspiration, illustrating the transformative power of resilience and determination. As you face challenges, remember that your journey is uniquely yours, and every hurdle is a chance to emerge stronger.

6. **Nurturing Your Entrepreneurial Vision:**
Chapter 6 guided you in crafting your business vision, from developing a comprehensive business plan to understanding the critical role of market research. Your vision is not just a goal; it's the North Star guiding your entrepreneurial expedition. With a well-crafted vision, you are poised for sustained success and fulfillment.

7. **Cultivating Your Entrepreneurial Tribe:**
Chapter 7 explored the pivotal facet of building your support network. Whether it's curating a dynamic team, fostering relationships with partners and vendors, or infusing determination into relationship building, your entrepreneurial tribe forms the foundation for collaborative success.

8. **Elevating Your Sales and Marketing Mastery:**
Chapter 8 immersed us in the indispensable realms of mastering sales and marketing. Understanding your target audience, crafting compelling value propositions, and deploying effective marketing strategies are pivotal in attracting and retaining customers. Remember, sales and marketing are not just tools but instruments in your entrepreneurial repertoire.

9. **Navigating the Heights - Scaling and Expanding Your Business:**
   In Chapter 9, we plunged into the exhilarating yet intricate process of scaling and expanding your business. Scaling marks a pivotal milestone in your entrepreneurial odyssey, and your determination, resource mastery, and adaptation to global ventures are the keys to navigating this transformative phase.

10. **Crafting Your Entrepreneurial Legacy:**
    Chapter 10 concludes our journey by unraveling the concept of the entrepreneurial legacy. It's not just about financial success but your impact on your industry, community, and future entrepreneurs. Succession planning, mentorship, and values transference are the tools that shape a legacy beyond business.

    As you close this book, remember that your entrepreneurial journey is an ongoing odyssey filled with learning, growth, and pursuing your passions. The challenges you face are not roadblocks but opportunities for innovation. The triumphs you achieve are personal victories and contributions to the broader entrepreneurial landscape.

    Embrace your role as an entrepreneur with determination, resilience, and a commitment to leaving a legacy of impact. The odyssey continues, and the pages of your entrepreneurial story are waiting to be written. May your journey be filled with success, fulfillment, and a lasting legacy that transcends generations. Onward, entrepreneur, to new horizons!

AUTHOR'S TIPS AND TRICKS

- Mindset, Perspective, Insights: Emphasizing the importance of cultivating a positive and growth-oriented mindset, gaining valuable perspectives, and seeking insights.

- Focus: Stressing the need for concentration and avoiding distractions to achieve specific goals.

- Commitment: Highlighting the significance of dedication and unwavering commitment to one's objectives.

- Time/Dedication: Acknowledging the role of time management and dedicated efforts in achieving success.

- Habit: Recognizing habits and discipline as foundational elements for success and the importance of establishing routines.

- Never Give Up, take a Break: Encourage persistence and resilience, but acknowledge the importance of taking breaks when needed.

- Think Outside the Box: Promoting creativity, innovation, and unconventional thinking to stand out from competitors.

- Self-improvement, Betterment, or Confidence: Advocating continuous improvement, innovation, and building self-confidence.

- Moral/Ethics/Principle/Integrity: Stressing the importance of maintaining high ethical standards and principles.

- Change: Embracing change as a constant factor and adapting to new circumstances.

- Cultural/Norm: Understanding and respecting cultural

norms in business and life.

- Handle Rejection: Building resilience to handle and use rejection as a learning opportunity.

- Game-Changing Strategy/Operations: Developing innovative and effective strategies to bring about significant change.

- Company-Tangible and Intangible Asset: Recognizing both tangible and intangible assets as valuable for a company's success.

- Adaptation/Change: Emphasizing the need for adaptability and the ability to navigate changes.

- Flexibility: Staying flexible in approach and operations to meet evolving challenges.

- Transformation, Maintain Growth, and Development: Continuously evolving and growing to stay relevant in a changing environment.

- Resilience: Building the capacity to bounce back from setbacks and challenges.

- Take Challenge: Encouraging individuals to embrace challenges as opportunities for growth.

- Handle Objection: Developing skills to handle objections and turn them into opportunities.

- Follow-Up: Recognizing the importance of consistent follow-up in business and relationships.

- Attitude, Manner, Vibe: The significance of maintaining a positive attitude, professional demeanor, and positive energy.

- Character: A strong and ethical character is important in personal and professional life.

- Communication: Emphasizing effective communication skills as crucial for success.

- People Skills/Work with People: Highlighting the importance of interpersonal skills and collaboration.

- Consistency: The need for consistency in efforts and actions.

- Belief: Believing in oneself and one's capabilities.

- Personality: The role of personality in shaping one's approach to life and business.

- Philosophy: Developing a personal philosophy that aligns with goals and values.

- Self-Improvement, Effective, Efficiency: Continuous focus on personal development, effectiveness, and efficiency.

- Motivation/Drive: Maintaining motivation and a strong drive to achieve goals.

- Negotiation Skill: Building effective negotiation skills for business and personal interactions.

Collectively, these tips provide a holistic perspective on the qualities and strategies needed for success in various aspects of life and business.

Index:

www.ingramcontent.com/pod-product-compliance
Lightning Source LLC
Chambersburg PA
CBHW060046210326
41520CB00009B/1284